Performance Management
in
Local Government

by

Steve Rogers

General Editors: Michael Clarke and John Stewart

LONGMAN

in association with the Local Government Training Board

Published by Longman Industry and Public Service Management, Longman Group UK Ltd, 6th Floor, Westgate House, The High, Harlow, Essex CM20 1YR, UK.

Telephone Harlow (0279) 442601
Fax (0279) 444501

First published 1990

British Library Cataloguing in Publication Data
Rogers, Stephen
   Performance Management. – (Longman and Local
   Government Training Board Series).
   1. Great Britain. Local Government. Management
   I. Title   II. Series
   352.041

ISBN 0–582–06248–9

Phototypeset by Input Typesetting Ltd, London
Printed and bound in Great Britain by
Biddles Ltd, Guildford and King's Lynn

Contents

Other titles in the series

Human Resource Management in Local Government
by *Alan Fowler*

Marketing in Local Government
by *Kieron Walsh*

Organising for Local Government: a local political responsibility
by *John Barratt and John Downs*

Planning for Change: strategic planning in local government
by *Ian Caulfield and John Schulz*

Understanding the Management of Local Government: its special purposes, conditions and tasks
by *John Stewart*

Managing the Enabling Authority
by *Rodney Brooke*

Financial Management in the 1990s
by *David Rawlinson and Brian Tanner*

General Management in Local Government: getting the balance right
by *Michael Clarke and John Stewart*

Preface

Performance Management is a phrase which can be interpreted broadly or narrowly. It can be used to describe a specific management system or it can be an all-embracing term covering virtually all aspects of management. It may be seen as relevant only to the staff of local authorities or as involving councillors and citizens. It has no single definition which is universally accepted.

In writing this book I have therefore had to determine the way in which I wish to use the phrase and to decide what should be included and what left out. In doing this I am aware that any definition and choices will not meet with agreement from all readers, but that is inevitable. Local government management is changing rapidly and as it does the concepts, ideas and words which are used are in a state of constant evolution. The purpose of this book is not to try to impose universal and fixed definitions, for change and variety are valuable characteristics in local government. My choices are therefore personal ones.

For the purposes of this book I will define Performance Management in the following terms as the interrelated processes which ensure that:

▽ all the activities and people in a local authority contribute as effectively as possible to its objectives

▽ all activities and objectives are systematically reviewed in a way which enables a local authority to learn and thereby to improve its service to the community.

The definition is a broad one, being based on a view that the 'performance' of a local authority must include not just what it does but also what it achieves as a result of its activity. Managing 'performance' must therefore include not only the management of action but also the management of evaluation.

The broad scope of the definition I have used means that some degree of selectivity has been necessary. In presenting the issues and ideas which I believe to be of the greatest importance I am keenly aware of having omitted other important aspects of the topic. In particular I have not attempted to deal with the specific techniques which have been developed to evaluate and assess individual local authority services. There are now so many and they deserve more detailed exploration and analysis than can be provided here. Nor, for the same reasons, have I included reference to the techniques used by auditors.

When writing about management there is always a danger of falling into the trap of making vague exhortations about the need for better management. There is also the danger of presenting apparently simple solutions to complex problems without explaining the subtleties they really involve. While I have tried to avoid these traps it is unlikely that I have been completely successful. My main intention however, has been to provoke thought rather than to prescribe solutions.

A number of examples from particular local authorities have been used in some chapters and I am grateful to those authorities for allowing me to use them. They are briefly presented and I hope I have done justice to them and to the people involved in creating them. They are not intended as models for other local authorities simply to copy for they have all evolved from their own particular local context and inevitably I have not been able to describe that context in any detail. I am grateful to those authorities, and to the many others I could have used, in a quite different sense, for they represent the very positive and creative approach which so many local authorities have adopted at a time of increasing criticism and complaint. Those positive, but different responses are an indication of the many strengths of local government.

Dedication

The Institute of Local Government Studies is unusual in the way it successfully manages to bring together the often separate worlds of academics and
practitioners. For anyone who is fascinated by local government it is a
remarkable place and I consider myself fortunate to work there. The many
local government officers and councillors who attend the Institute each year
have been a constant source of ideas and challenge. I am indebted to many
of them. I am also indebted to many of my colleagues at the Institute who,
whether they realize it or not, have influenced my thinking and supported
and encouraged me.

Finally, and most importantly I wish to thank my family, Carolyn,
Ben, Nicky and Lizzie for their constant love and support and for allowing
me, during the many hours spent writing this book, to neglect my responsibilities as husband and parent.

Steve Rogers
Birmingham
July 1990

1 A new focus on performance

Introduction

The circumstances within which local authorities are managed have changed significantly during the past decade. The changes have been dramatic – and sometimes traumatic. Their impact on the way in which local authority services are provided and managed has, in many respects, been greater than that resulting from the reorganisation of local government in the 1960's and 1970's. On reflecting on these changes, it is tempting to conclude that they are entirely the consequence of central government legislation and pressure, for it is clearly central government which has forced the pace of change not only in local government, but in the public sector generally. But that would be too simplistic a conclusion and one which would fail to acknowledge the many changes and developments undertaken by individual local authorities in order to improve their performance – whether that be as a corporate entity, or in terms of their specific services, or in relation to their individual employees.

In attempting to review the ways in which local authorities are trying to improve the management of their performance, the extent and diversity of developments and innovations is quite dazzling – something to which this book cannot hope to do justice. It is quite clear that local authorities are not simply responding to the requirements of central government to become more accountable or to be more economic and efficient – in some cases they have gone beyond the basic requirements. Other local authorities have moved in different directions by, for example, developing new forms of relationship with their electorate and customers. In many local authorities there have been examples of innovation as they struggle to resolve the conflict which frequently exists between central government demands and local demands and needs.

The changes which have and are taking place have created considerable interest in the concept of performance, and as a consequence the vocabulary of local government management has been filled with phrases beginning with that word – performance review, performance appraisal and performance indicators being but a few examples. This is in stark contrast to the situation which existed in the past when the only time the word 'performance' appeared on a committee agenda was when a council had its periodic debate on whether or not it should have a Performance Review Sub-Committee.

Before proceeding to examine what some of the phrases associated with performance mean, and how systems and procedures for managing performance have been developed, it is necessary to understand the main changing pressures and new forms of thinking which have led to this upsurge in interest in the topic. Their combined impact, both inside and outside of local government, has created a new set of values and expectations on which many of the new systems and procedures for managing performance are based.

Legislative pressures

The almost constant flow of legislation during the 1980's has markedly changed the conditions and circumstances within which a local authority performs. The programme of legislation has achieved major reforms in the political organisation of local authorities, in member-officer relations and in local government finance. It has created major changes with regard to competition and consumer choice, and in so doing has raised major issues and concerns about the present and future role of local government in society. Some of these changes have been achieved through major reforms of specific areas of service such as education, social services, housing, land-use planning, economic development and waste management – reforms which have redefined the local authority role, its activities and approach to management.

Faced with having to interpret and implement such extensive change, local authorities have responded in a variety of ways. At one extreme, they have adopted a minimalist approach, attempting to conform to the requirements of the legislation, while keeping the overall shape and approach to policy making and management as unchanged as possible. In some cases, this may have been achieved satisfactorily in the short term, but there are indications that such an approach may create longer term problems of lack of clarity and understanding of roles, relationships, structures and procedures. At the other extreme there are local authorities which are undertaking a more fundamental appraisal of their role and management arrangements, which has involved 'rewriting the book of local government'.

In undertaking this appraisal, it has been necessary for them to identify the main themes which emerge from the legislation and it is clear that with regard to local authority performance there are five dominant themes.

1 Accountability

The Government has sought to make local authorities more accountable to their electorates by means of a range of measures which include:

▽ the requirement on local authorities to publish Annual Reports
▽ the requirement to publish specific information in the fields of housing and schools provision
▽ the opening of meetings to the public and press
▽ the requirement to appoint a finance officer and a monitoring officer with statutory duties regarding the local authority's conduct
▽ the change in the basis of local taxation from a property tax to a poll

tax in order to create a more direct relationship between a local authority's financial performance and the financial burden placed on a larger
number of local tax-payers.

Whether the Government's aims in creating greater accountability have
or will be fully achieved is open to some doubt. The creation of the
community charge as a mechanism for achieving local accountability
appears, at the moment at least, to be of uncertain efficacy, having become
inextricably confused with the Government's greater aim of controlling
the individual and aggregate expenditure of local authorities. Nonetheless,
whatever the longer term impact of the community charge on local accountability, the combined effect of the various legislative measures has been
considerable, requiring local authorities to give much closer attention to
the way in which they present themselves to their citizens and customers,
and to the way in which they define what they mean by their 'performance'.

The Government has also successfully achieved its pursuit of greater
accountability by means of the establishment of the Audit Commission in
1983. Created in part to take over the former District Audit's auditing
functions, it was required, as were other auditors used by local authorities,
to ensure that proper arrangements were made for securing economy,
efficiency and effectiveness – more broadly interpreted as being to ensure
wise and prudent administration. But it is in its wider role of providing
advice and analysis for local government generally that its impact in achieving accountability has been of greatest significance. In particular, its work
in defining and refining performance measures, and its use of them to
compare the performance of local authorities has created a widespread
interest.

The Commission has been regarded as both friend and foe by local
authorities – there is a love-hate relationship which stems inevitably from
its twin role of watchdog and adviser. While the Commission has demonstrated its desire and ability to assist local authorities, particularly through
the numerous special studies which it has undertaken, there has been more
room for conflict and disagreement over the way the Commission has tended
to focus primarily on issues of economy and efficiency in its approach to
performance measurement and inter-authority comparisons – an approach
considered by many people in local authorities to have distorted and limited
the analysis of local government performance in both the public and political domains. In defence of the Audit Commission, it must be stated that
it has for several years publicly acknowledged the need to give greater
attention to Effectiveness – the missing 3rd 'E' in its remit – and its recent
creation of a Quality Exchange is, at the very least, an omen of good
intent.

The Audit Commission is only one of several bodies which perform
an auditing and inspectional role over local authority services – for example,
education, social services and the police all have their own inspection
agencies, and it is noticeable that some of these agencies have considerably
extended the range and nature of their activities. The Social Services
Inspectorate in the Department of Health is a good example of this process,
having in recent years impressively transformed its role in the direction of

providing advice, analysis and guidelines for social services committees and departments.

2 Choice

The legislative programme has extended the right and ability of the customers of local authority services to choose whether they want those services to continue to be provided by local government or by another agency. This is expressed most clearly in the legislation permitting parents and tenants to opt out of local authority provision of education and housing management services. Choice is an extension of the principle of accountability. In the past customers have had the right to be informed about the performance of local authority services so that they could evaluate and make judgments about them, but their ability to make their judgments count, for them to have influence and effect, has been limited by the effectiveness of mechanisms such as voting in elections, participating in party political processes and in local and national pressure groups and community groups – and by complaining. To this range of mechanisms has been added the clear right of choice.

3 Competition – for customers

Through the creation of agencies such as Housing Action Trusts and City Technology Colleges, the Government has placed local authorities in a position where they have, in a sense, to compete for customers. In addition to creating new agencies the Government has also required and encouraged the involvement of the private sector in issues such as inner city regeneration and economic development, which had previously been regarded as lying within the exclusive domain of local government, or at least as issues where local government was perceived to have the dominant role.

In many cases this involvement was intended to be achieved through a process of partnership, but in other cases, the aim appears to have been to by-pass the local authority. The Government has also given encouragement and support to the 'third arm' of public provision, the voluntary sector, the results of which are most obviously demonstrated in the growth of housing associations as major providers of rented housing.

In all these cases the effect has been to provide an alternative model of funding, decision-making and service provision against which the performance of local authorities can be directly or indirectly compared. The agencies which have grown or been created are therefore in many senses competitors with the local authority for their customers. Customers are placed more and more in a market situation where they may be able to choose between different providers of goods and services, and in exercising their choice will, by implication, make judgments about the performance of the goods and services on offer.

4 Competition – for work

The requirement to put services out to competitive tender has forced local authorities to think clearly and precisely about how to define 'performance' with respect to the management and delivery of services. Faced with the possibility of losing direct control of service provision they have had to determine specific answers to questions such as:

▽ How do we want the contractor to perform?
▽ How can we specify service standards?
▽ How can the contractor's performance be measured, inspected and evaluated?
▽ How can deficient performance be controlled and improved?
▽ What sanctions or penalties can be used against contractors who continue not to perform adequately?

Compulsory competitive tendering, by clearly distinguishing the role of client from that of contractor, has focused local authority attention on a range of performance issues to a degree and in a way which often did not exist when local authorities automatically provided the same services themselves.

The sharpened focus on performance has not been restricted just to those services which have been directly subjected to competition. Its wider effects have been felt in a number of ways:

▽ the open-ended nature of the legislation which allows the government to extend the range of services subject to it (as they quickly did in the case of leisure services) has persuaded local authorities to prepare other services by making them more 'competitive'
▽ the rigours of having to work under competitive conditions have led many managers in DLO's and DSO's to question the overhead costs their services have to pay to those central departments which provide financial, legal, personnel and other support services. In a competitive situation the effective management of overhead costs can be as important as managing direct costs and therefore managers have been keen to ensure that they receive 'value for money' for those services. This has resulted in a shift of attitudes, relative power and procedures in some local authorities which are now examining in much greater depth the questions of cost and quality of central support services. This has resulted in a range of developments which include service level agreements, the privatization of support services and the introduction of time-based work measurement systems so that costs can be allocated on the basis of actual service provided.
▽ at a more discrete level competitive tendering has also focused attention on the problems of performance measurement. While contracting out makes the need for adequate and appropriate measures of performance more urgent, it generally does not make their generation or use any easier. It may be argued that the fears expressed by local authorities as to whether they can adequately monitor the performance of contractors of certain kinds of service stem from their knowledge and recognition of the considerable inadequacies of the performance measures

available to them. Competitive tendering has, however, opened up new avenues of thinking and has changed attitudes towards the whole issue of performance measurement.

5 Employment conditions

The relative stability of employment conditions which has been characteristic of local government in the past has been challenged by several items of legislation. Of direct impact is the legislation relating to competitive tendering and opting out which directly challenges the assumption of continuing, long-term employment by local authority. It has also focused attention on the full costs of permanent employment and has been a factor influencing the use of term contracts, particularly for chief officers, although this has also been influenced by the increasing tendency to adopt private sector management practices in local government. More generally, employment legislation and the reduction in power and influence of trade unions has created a shift in the legal basis of the relationship between employer and employee. Some local authorities have taken advantage of this change by themselves reducing the role and status of trade unions, by removing restrictive practices and by introducing more open-ended contracts of employment, which can be more freely interpreted by managers. Other local authorities have been more equivocal in their attitude to these changes and some have deliberately maintained the role and status of trade unions and preserved employment conditions in pursuit of their aim of being a 'model employer'.

Whichever approach has been taken it is apparent that the legislation has created opportunities for local authorities to adopt a range of solutions to some of their perceived problems relating to the performance of their employees. The extent to which these solutions are accepted by a majority of their employees, as against the extent to which they are perceived as punitive measures imposed upon them, will, in the longer term, constitute an important criterion by which the success of many recent 'Performance Management Systems' may be judged.

Changing philosophies and styles of management

During the 1980's a remarkable shift in the philosophies and styles of management began to occur in local government and elsewhere in the public sector. The shift was characterized by a breakdown in the barriers of thinking which had previously existed between much of the public and private sectors. Whereas previously private sector philosophies, styles and procedures of management were often looked on with suspicion by many local government managers and councillors, during the 1980's an almost direct reversal of this way of thinking could be observed with at least some local government managers looking to the private sector for models of good management. The causes of this change are of some complexity but there are several developments which played a significant part.

First, there was the concern which had been first voiced over twenty years ago that local government management was in danger of becoming too 'inbred' and the suggested solution was to import more senior managers from the private sector and elsewhere in the public sector. It was a solution more talked about than practised, for relatively few senior managers were so imported and some of them departed fairly rapidly; but it was a sign of a gradually changing culture and climate – a window which had been opened on a different world of management.

Of greater significance has been the attitude and style of the Government, and of Mrs. Thatcher in particular. Firmly believing that public sector management was in need of radical reform and that much could be learnt from the best of the private sector, she personally appointed captains of industry such as Sir Derek Rayner of Marks and Spencer and Sir Roy Griffiths of Sainsburys, to undertake major investigations and reforms of public sector organization and management practices. In addition her own style of political leadership was put forward by some supporters and commentators as a model of how best to achieve a radical overhaul of the public sector.

But perhaps the development of greatest significance was the emergence in the early 1980's of what was to become a whole new library of management literature. Based on the theme of Excellence, and starting with 'In Search of Excellence' by Tom Peters and Robert Waterman, the literature contained a set of principles which have had a remarkable effect on managers in all sectors of the economy and in many parts of the world. Many of the identified attributes of excellence were quickly perceived to be of relevance to local government but the theme of *close to the customer* has had a particularly dramatic impact, both directly and by means of its development and extension into the 'Public Service Orientation' literature initiated by Michael Clarke and John Stewart.

Whilst the PSO and close to the customer themes are of direct relevance to the question of managing performance, three other attributes of excellence have been important in influencing the way some local authorities have introduced performance management:

▽ *A Bias for Action* is an attribute which has several themes written into it, but of central importance is the concept of results-oriented activity. It is expressed in the language of 'do it, try it, fix it', of tangible achievements and results-first management. It is about identifying specific short-term objectives and it requires an attitude which is more concerned with problem-solving than issue analysis. It is a philosophy which underpins the performance management systems, business systems and performance appraisal systems which some local authorities have developed in recent years. One fundamental aim of these systems is to ensure things happen, that intended achievements are specified and results produced. They use the language of 'action plans', 'targets' and 'achievements'. It is an approach which probably appears alien and uncomfortable to those whose philosophy of management has remained unchanged, but for others it is a refreshing antidote to the frustration caused by endless discussions, fruitless meetings and lack of both direction and sense of achievement.

▽ *Productivity through People*. The realization that employees are a local authority's most important resource, the ultimate source of all quality and productivity improvements, was hardly new. What was new was the acceptance that local authorities needed to reflect more clearly that belief in the importance of their employees rather than simply pay lip-service to it, and that has caused local authorities to become more creative in developing their procedures for managing people and in overcoming some of the barriers which had previously existed. Better communications, clearer allocation of responsibility, new pay scales and financial rewards and greater provision of training and development opportunities have all been introduced as means of reflecting the belief in the value of employees.

▽ *Simultaneous Loose-Tight Properties*. The recognition that it is important for an organization to retain tight control over things which really matter but to exercise only loose control over less important matters has been an important change in philosophy in organizations such as local authorities which in the past have often appeared to be dominated by the need to control everything. Past traditions of accountability have emphasized the need for detailed controls, but those controls have often not been effective and have had the additional cost of preventing innovation and initiative. The process of loosening the reins of detailed control has forced local authorities to analyse what is important and therefore needs to be managed tightly, and that process has been of great benefit in helping them to identify a sense of purpose and direction.

Decentralized and devolved management

Many local authorities spent the early years after reorganization in trying to create a sense of unity and corporateness. In many cases this resulted in a dominant need to achieve uniformity in service provision and in an excessive degree of central control over line managers. Concern with these tendencies began to be expressed at the political level as it became recognized that some forms of centralized decision-making were unable to respond to or reflect the variety of local needs and expectations within the authority. This resulted in some local authorities adopting a variety of patterns of political decentralization, but the impact has been more widely felt at managerial and service delivery levels within local authorities where there have been considerable movements to decentralize geographically and to devolve management decision-making to responsibility centres or cost centres.

Devolved or cost-centre management is particularly relevant to performance in so far as it involves giving managers greater autonomy and freedom to make decisions and allocate resources within a framework of clear guidelines, defined budgets, specific objectives and explicit performance targets. Its success is dependent upon the ability of senior managers to provide a framework of expectations so that they can release the reins of detailed, day-to-day controls without losing overall strategic direction of what is done and what is achieved. Devolved management as a consequence highlights many of the key issues involved in understanding how performance can be managed, of which the following are particularly relevant:

▽   the need for a hierarchy of expectations, ranging from strategic aims to specific action targets
▽   the need for clear identification of accountabilities, responsibilities and scope for discretion and their allocation to individual managers at all levels within the management hierarchy.
▽   the need for systematic monitoring and performance review – including the specification of performance standards and performance measures and the use of staff appraisal.
▽   the underlying need for better management information systems which provide the information required by all levels of management in order for them to fulfil their responsibilities while remaining accountable for their actions. The use of information technology has, as a consequence, been critical to the success of schemes for devolving management responsibility downwards.

The quest for quality

'Quality' was not a word which was in very frequent use in local government management until very recently. Its relative absence may simply have arisen as a result of the dominance achieved by the 'three E's' – economy, efficiency and effectiveness – as a way of describing performance. Although, theoretically, the concept of quality is implicitly included within the 'three E's', the language had the effect of obscuring what now appears to be a word which has meaning for service providers, managers, councillors and the public. 'Quality of service' as a basis for thinking about performance has a widespread popular appeal and is likely to become the prime moving force in creating improvements in performance during the next decade.

The emerging concern with quality can be traced to five different sources:

▽   Compulsory competitive tendering – which forced local authorities to become much more explicit about the standards of service required of contractors. Quality, together with quantity and cost became an important item in contract documents, replacing the earlier language of effectiveness, outputs and outcomes.
▽   Models of private sector practice – local authorities began to use the language and concepts of quality adopted in the private sector. For example Total Quality Management, Quality Circles, Quality Assurance and Quality Control have all been converted and adopted for public sector use.
▽   A reaction to the dominance of economy and efficiency – a decade of focusing primarily on these aspects of performance has inevitably led to an increasing public, political, managerial and professional concern with the effect on the quality of services delivered. That concern found expression more easily in the concept of quality than in the missing third 'E' of effectiveness – a concept which was not so readily understood and defined.
▽   Customer orientation. The developing focus on the customer, coupled with a more articulate and vocal public response to local authority services, demonstrated that there was a public concern not just with

the quantity and cost of services, but also with their quality. Moreover, the increasing use of satisfaction surveys began to demonstrate that the public were quite capable of differentiating between different levels of service quality and were able to apply their own criteria as to what they meant by quality. The awareness that this information created in local authorities helped counter the defensive bureaucratic and political arguments sometimes put forward that the public did not know, did not understand and did not care, and opened the way for a more serious analysis of customer-oriented quality issues.

▽   A new political focus on quality was provided within the Labour Party with the publication of 'Quality Street'. Using quality as the central concept around which improvements would be made to management and service delivery, it contained ideas such as quality audits, a Quality Commission and customer contracts, some of which have subsequently been developed by local authorities to stimulate improvements in services.

Quality now provides a potentially powerful focus for political and managerial thinking about performance and its impact is already being felt in some local authorities. There is, however, a danger that 'quality' can simply become a rhetorical buzzword, used as a promotional gimmick as it sometimes is in the private sector, rather than as a dynamic agent for analysing, designing and reviewing service provision. It may, therefore, in the 1990's achieve the status of the phrase 'value for money' in the 1980's, which was used both as a relatively meaningless symbol and as the driving force behind many important improvements in performance. 'Quality', if it is to become more than a promotional gimmick, needs to be translated into specific criteria which can be used by councillors, managers and the public. There are clear signs that this is happening already.

New roles for local government

The Government's legislative programme, because of its radical nature, and also because it has been perceived by some as an attack on local government, has had the effect of stimulating debate and consideration of the role of local government and the nature of local democracy.

The debate has become most clearly focused around three concepts or definitions of the role of local authorities – enabling, partnership, and regulation and inspection. All three concepts now provide a necessary counter-balance to the previously dominant role of service provider. The enabling debate is wide-ranging for there are quite different views of what is meant by 'enabling', ranging from Nicholas Ridley's minimalist view of local government's role as a direct provider to the broader view of enabling and community government expressed by writers such as Clarke, Stewart and Stoke. In both views of 'enabling', however, it is clear that direct service provision is only one of several means of providing services for the public which local authorities need to consider. The concept of enabling has had the effect of requiring politicians and managers to consider not only the question . . .

'How can we best run our services?'
but also the question . . .
'How, and by whom, should local services best be provided?'

Partnership is a concept which can be subsumed within the enabling debate, but is worthy of separate identification because it has found practical expression in a variety of central government initiatives, such as the regeneration of inner city areas and collaboration with health authorities. The importance of concepts of enabling and partnership for the performance of local authorities lies in the fact that both concepts introduce new criteria by which a local authority's performance needs to be judged. Achievements such as the ability to influence, negotiate, stimulate, encourage and support activities which are beyond its direct control became as important in determining successful performance as is the ability directly to provide services which are economical, efficient and effective. Making judgments in these kinds of terms is likely to prove more difficult and there is a danger that, as a consequence, they will not achieve adequate attention. In some local authorities there may also remain greater emphasis placed on the Audit Commission's concept of the Competitive Council, with its emphasis on competing and contracting, rather than on a partnership or enabling model of the local authority's role.

Regulation and inspection have been traditional roles performed by local authorities and are central to the work of departments such as Environmental Health and Consumer Protection. But such departments are usually small and their activities have in the past rarely been at the top of local authorities' political and managerial agendas, which have been dominated by issues of service provision and resource allocation in the main service departments. Despite the central role played by environmental health in the historical development of local government, in recent years the attitude of some local authorities to its role can best be described as ambivalent, an attitude which is also reflected in other regulatory and inspectoral functions which exist as small sections in large departments, which are otherwise concerned with the direct provision of services. Nowhere is this better represented than in many Social Services departments, where inspection units have often been isolated from, and without influence on, the senior management of the department. Perhaps only in the area of development control has regulation remained a dominant issue of political concern.

Change has already occurred and regulation and inspection has begun to achieve a much higher profile within local government. In part this has been stimulated by government legislation, especially in areas such as education and social services, where the local authority's role has become more clearly defined in terms of planning and monitoring services – but not necessarily directly providing them. But stimulus has also resulted from a much greater public and political concern with the physical environment not just with regard to 'green issues' but with a broad range of matters which are recognized as influencing the quality of urban and rural life.

In search of performance in the 1990's

The trends in the management and organization of local authority services which have developed in the 1980's have already had many beneficial effects but they can also have potentially damaging implications. For example, the growing emphasis on action and results, on getting the job done, has been an extremely positive force in improving the performance of local authority services. But there is a danger that if the concern for short-term results, for economy and efficiency, becomes the dominant and exclusive way of judging the performance of local authorities, then the role of local government, and of the political process, becomes devalued. Collecting refuse is an important service and it is equally important that it is done efficiently and at the lowest possible cost. But there are a wider set of values inherent in local government – public service is not just about the efficient delivery of services.

The movement towards greater clarity of purpose and direction which has been demonstrated by central government and by many local authorities has been beneficial in ensuring that results are achieved. But there is a danger that 'providing a sense of direction' can become translated into crude forms of coercion and control and more autocratic styles of management. Councillors and officers in local government are keenly aware of the extent to which central government has successfully imposed its values on local government, and in so doing, has effectively altered the balance of power in central-local relations. Within local authorities, councillors and senior managers appear to have drawn some important conclusions from the political and managerial style of the Government. Many local authorities in the past were characterised by an immense diffusion of power, with many different stakeholders appearing to have a hand on the tiller. The extent of diffusion often resulted in a degree of confusion and inactivity which was indefensible. In the 1980's a number of local authorities have sought to correct that situation and have used concepts of performance management, amongst other mechanisms, to achieve a greater unity of values, purpose and direction. There is a danger that such mechanisms, while removing confusion and inactivity, can produce political and managerial processes which are less democratic, less pluralistic and less participative.

The challenge for the 1990's lies in the extent to which local authorities can successfully maintain their emerging focus on achieving purpose, direction and action, whilst at the same time ensuring that it is achieved in as democratic and participative a way as possible. Pursuing these twin goals will not be easy, for there are many areas of potential conflict, but there are already many signs that local authorities are attempting to do so. The mechanisms being used are immensely variable – consumer surveys, customer contracts, more realistic planning mechanisms, devolved management, and more rigorous and sensitive performance appraisals and review procedures are but a few examples. They all signify that a continuing analysis of how a local authority can improve its performance is under way.

Questions

▲
  What are the most important external factors which have influenced the way performance is managed in your own local authority?
▲ *What have been the most significant changes in thinking about performance in your local authority?*
▲ *What are the key issues you will need to consider in the next three years?*

2 Performance – some terms and concepts

Defining terms

The language of performance management is in many ways already well developed and it could be assumed that most of the terms used are well understood and clearly defined. Unfortunately that does not appear to be the case, for numerous words and phrases are used interchangeably without clear definition and, on occasion, without clear understanding. The lack of clarity may be partly ascribed to the fact that the language of performance management, like all language, is in a state of constant evolution, as new ideas and changing circumstances influence its use. It also results from the fact that the precise words and phrases used represent concepts which are drawn from different disciplines, professions and groups. The language is that of politics, economics, accountancy, and management theory and the words used by politicians, economists, personnel practitioners and service professions may sound the same but they do not always have the same meaning.

Within the context of evolving meanings the following 'glossary of terms' cannot hope to impose a uniformity of definition. It can however clarify some of the different usages of the more common terms in use, and the terms are therefore grouped to represent the main areas of overlap.

1 Inputs, outputs and outcomes

Within the concept of the three E's definition of performance (see below) there is a reasonable measure of agreement as to the meaning of these terms. Inputs refer to the resources, which are used to produce a service or execute a policy and are expressed in terms of finance, personnel, equipment etc. Outputs refers to the services produced or delivered. They are most often expressed in terms of their quantity but should also include some statement of quality. Outcome is the term most variably defined but is generally considered to be a statement of what actually happens as a result of providing the service or of the benefits of the service to its users. This definition can sometimes conflict with the use of the term 'Impact' which may be described as the ultimate effect of a policy, both intended and unintended.

The use of the term 'inputs' in the sense described above is a narrow one and does not take into account the fact that, for many services, the inputs to a service cannot be limited to resources alone but must also include the characteristics or needs of those customers or clients for whom the service is provided. Thus, in education, it is appropriate to consider pupil characteristics as an input to the educational process.

2 Economy, efficiency and effectiveness

Economy, in the sense used by the Audit Commission, means minimising the cost of acquiring a given set of resources such as staff, equipment and premises. Traditionally the focus of economy was therefore on activities such as bulk purchasing arrangements and ensuring that staff costs were kept to a minimum, but attention has now shifted to the use of contracting out and leasing as methods for achieving economy. More broadly, and perhaps more commonly, economy is used to mean reducing or minimising the total expenditure of a local authority or service.

Efficiency is the relationship between inputs (i.e. resources used) and outputs (i.e. services produced). Greater efficiency is achieved either by increasing the outputs from a given level of input (by, for example, productivity improvement programmes) or reducing the inputs required to produce a given output (by, for example, cost reduction exercises).

Effectiveness is usually defined as the relationship between outputs and outcomes and, more precisely, as the extent to which policy objectives are achieved. The limitation of this definition is that it is concerned primarily with the intended effects of a policy, whereas it may be argued that unintended effects can be of equal importance.

3 Values, aims, objectives and targets

The terms in this group are now used so interchangeably as to defy common definition. They are all however statements of *intent* or *expectation*, with values being at the highest and therefore most general level and targets representing the more precise and specific statements. Values and aims, and sometimes the term 'mission', are used the most interchangeably, reflecting the beliefs which are held by the local authority or the broad characteristics that it would wish to see represented in its policies and activities. The following example is an indication of the level at which they may be set:

Give all customers the best possible service.
Ensure quality and value for money.
Identify and respond to changing needs.
Achieve partnership with the local community.
Care for the disadvantaged.
Pursue equality of opportunity.
Look after and listen to staff.
Protect and improve the environment.
Increase the prosperity of all residents.
(Bolton Metro: Agenda for the 90's)

Objectives may be stated in a variety of ways but normally are precise statements of the achievements to be fulfilled in meeting aims. They can be categorized as immediate, intermediate and final, or in terms of impact (i.e. those having a specific effect or outcome), service (i.e. those which define ways that changes may be brought about) and logistical (i.e. those which enable the service to be carried out). The use of the words objectives and targets may also overlap, with the latter tending to be more highly quantified and related to specific activities and events. They may also reflect specific timescales, levels of efficiency and quality specifications.

4 Performance measures and performance indicators

A distinction is often made between 'measures', as being precise and direct assessments of performance and 'indicators', as being more indirect assessments; i.e. they are only indicative of performance (N.B. for the sake of consistency, the term 'measures' will be used in the remainder of this book, except in those cases where examples from particular local authorities are being used).

5 Performance appraisal, performance review and performance management

The term 'appraisal' is used fairly consistently in relation to evaluations of the performance of individuals. Review is also used consistently to refer to the monitoring and evaluation of organizational performance. Performance management is used more variably and may sometimes be equated with performance appraisal, but on other occasions is used in the sense that it is in this book to include both individual and organizational performance it may be defined as an integrated set of planning and review procedures which cascade down through the organization to provide a link between each individual and the overall strategy of the organization.

6 Value for money

Value for money is of central importance to the concept of performance. It is a term which has achieved immense political, public and managerial importance as a symbolic phrase which has been used to promote and justify a wide range of reviews, reorganizations, cost reduction programmes and waste-cutting exercises. As with many symbolic statements, its use has been broad and sometimes ambiguous. It is rarely defined with precision but in practice has become more associated with economy and efficiency than with effectiveness, and hence the emphasis of its use has been more on money than on value.

Because of its practical usage in the past, it is now a symbol which is showing signs of its age. As a result, and because of its ambiguity and generality of meaning, it is a phrase which will not feature significantly in later chapters. Before dismissing this important phrase in such cavalier fashion, it is, however, worthy of some further examination in the light of the literal meaning of the words themselves.

'Value' is something which every individual places on the goods and services which they receive or purchase. Each will place a different value on the same service according to their individual preference and needs.

With respect to publicly provided goods and services, it is the essential role of government, local or national, to decide a common value on behalf of its citizens. That value will not be one with which all citizens agree nor is it likely to be the average of all their individual values. The purpose of the political process is to express value and exercise choice on behalf of the public generally. But public goods and services are not provided by governments comprising representatives who have a uniform set of values. Councillors, even within one political party, will vary considerably in the value they attach to particular services and they will inevitably be influenced by their managerial and professional advisors, who also have their own set of values, as will the staff who directly provide those services. In considering the concept of value, it therefore becomes essential to consider the question of *whose value* determines the provision of services and the allocation of resources.

Within the system of local government, there are many stakeholders who seek to exert their definition of value. They interact with each other in a complex and changing set of power relationships, which results in the need for a complex machinery of consultation, negotiation and decision making. In practice, the difficulties involved in resolving value conflicts can lead to an avoidance of explicit decisions. Each group of stakeholders then acts in an independent way.

The problem of value is also made more difficult by the complex nature of local government itself. In providing its many difficult services, a local authority must seek to achieve many different aims, not all of which are compatible, but amongst which it must achieve overall agreement. In recent years, there have been created a new set of solutions for resolving these questions of competing values. Within local authorities, there has been a movement towards achieving greater strategic direction and control by means of new systems of political and officer management which to some extent may be seen as representing a redistribution of power within local authorities. A second solution has been the introduction of principles of contract management, which also reflect a clear differentiation of power between the client, who specifies what is to be done, and the contractor, who has to perform that which is required in the contract.

The problem of competing values has also been tackled by moving some of the perceived sources of conflict beyond the boundary of the local authority. The use of outside contractors is one example, but of greater importance has been the removal of some functions and some types of decision from the direct control of the local authority. The process can be seen as one of simplification which is achieved through the reduction in the number of groups of direct stakeholders and the areas of choice to be exercised.

Value has to be related to money in situations of limited resources in order to become fully meaningful. Indeed, some commentators would argue that value has no meaning unless a price can be attached to it. Such thinking is also reflected in a number of the new solutions for achieving value for money and these include the introduction of price mechanisms for certain services, which bring with them the concept of individual choice for citizens and service users. This has the effect of transferring some elements of political choice to individuals, thereby reinforcing the concept that Value For Money is a matter of individual choice.

It may be argued that the consequence of much government legislation has been to move the pursuit of Value For Money in an entirely new direction for at least some local government services.

Accountability

The thinking represented in the preceding paragraphs in relation to Value For Money is also represented in the Government's approach to account-ability. In introducing the Community Charge, the Government has made clear that in its view local accountability depends essentially on the direct-ness of the relationship between paying for local services (through taxation) and voting in local elections. While that may be seen as a narrow definition of accountability, it is quite clearly a development of the individual choice theory.

There are two issues arising from this approach which require com-ment, the first of which is the confusion in the Government's own thinking. On the one hand, it is committed to maximising local choice and local accountability and, in that sense, welcomes variations between local author-ities as a means of providing comparisons and choice. On the other hand, it exhibits strong tendencies for central control which conflict with the concept of local accountability. Nowhere is this more amply demonstrated than in the way the community charge has been implemented.

The confused state of local accountability bears directly on the question of performance, for the two concepts are closely related. The Audit Com-mission clearly considers that accountability is the basis for performance review. In the introduction to its handbook on that subject, it justifies performance review in terms of achieving accountability:

> Performance review can enhance accountability by:
> 1 demonstrating success in achieving policy aims efficiently, economi-cally and effectively.
> 2 highlighting aspects of services where further enquiry and expla-nation is needed.
> 3 making the responsibilities and achievements of staff explicit.
> (Audit Commission: Performance Review in Local Government, 1986)

This statement leads to a further set of considerations. The concept of 'demonstrating' implies the need to make *information* available about per-formance – that is to provide an account of what has been done or achieved. The concept of accountability as the requirement to provide information is commonly used in relation to the provision of financial information, but the Audit Commission's definition implies more than that in so far as it refers to demonstrating effectiveness. It may be inferred from this that accountability must include an ability to demonstrate performance in the widest sense. The statement also raises the question of to whom an account should be given. The statement is set within a context of public account-ability but the reference to the responsibilities of staff presumably involves the concept of managerial accountability, for local government staff are not generally held to be directly accountable to the public – the accountability link is provided through elected representatives. Accountability in this sense involves a series of reporting relationships upwards through the tiers of staff of a local authority to its elected members and from them to the public.

Accountability involves more than the duty to report and the right to receive information: there is also the question of the right to exercise sanctions. Stewart (1984) defines these two different aspects of account-ability as a *link* of account and a *bond* of accountability. In the area of managerial accountability the bonds of accountability can be quite clear and precise, but in the areas of public accountability they have traditionally been relatively weak and reliance has been placed only on links. Ultimately the electoral process provides a bond of accountability but that is an imprecise bond. The position is now changing and some bonds of account-ability are being made clearer as in the case of education where there is now a clear bond of accountability between school head teachers and their governing bodies. The demands for greater public accountability are likely to result in an extension of such bonds and therefore a much greater scrutiny of the performance of local authorities.

Models for managing performance

If the concept of accountability is complex and if it is closely related to the concept of performance it may be assumed that performance also is complex. While that is undoubtedly true, it is an insufficient analysis for it does not lead to the identification of practical solutions.

Creating models or frameworks in order to classify complex situations can be a useful way of identifying possible solutions, although it is some-times a dangerous exercise if the models prove inadequate. The frameworks presented below are intended to prompt thinking about the different ways performance can be managed in a local authority rather than to represent comprehensive analyses of the subject.

Framework 1: The key performance problems of local government

The extent to which councillors and managers are prepared to under-take changes within their local authorities will depend on their analysis of the current level of performance and the pressures and requirements placed on them to do so. There has been no lack of criticism of local government management in recent years and some of the identified shortcomings are as follows:

▽ Lack of direction and sense of purpose.
▽ Lack of accountability – internally and externally.
▽ Lack of willingness to accept responsibility.
▽ Lack of action – too much deliberation, discussion and delay.
▽ Confusion of roles and responsibilities.
▽ Failure to respond to customers and citizens.
▽ Lack of a market mechanism to allocate resources.
▽ Lack of motivation to achieve.
▽ Excessively detailed controls and rules.

▽ Lack of appropriate incentives.
▽ Lack of information on which to base judgements and make decisions.
▽ Failure to quantify results explicitly.

There are many more such criticisms – you may wish to add your own and then identify which you believe to be the most important and relevant.

Framework 2: The principal organizational mechanisms for managing performance

While the management of performance may be complex, there are in fact a limited number of general mechanisms which organizations can use. These are:

1 PLANNING AND CONTROL SYSTEMS

In this context the use of the phrase 'planning and control' is intended to cover all those processes, procedures and structures which ensure that organizational purpose is made clear and transmitted throughout the organization, using a clear chain of command based on a clear specification of responsibility and accountability.

2 TECHNICAL SPECIFICATION AND STANDARDIZATION

The performance of some individual activities is managed through a process of detailed specification and codification which seeks to ensure that they are carried out in a uniform and standardised way.

3 PROFESSIONAL AND TECHNICAL COMPETENCE

Organizations use professional and craft union membership of their employees as a form of guarantee of the standard of work they perform and the ethical stance they will adopt.

4 MARKET MECHANISMS

Organizations use market mechanisms, which include the use of internal and external contracting to address directly the question of value for money.

5 ECONOMIC MECHANISMS

These mechanisms are concerned with the control of financial rewards and sanctions and include the use of financial incentives for staff and financial penalty clauses in contracts.

6 HUMAN RESOURCE MECHANISMS

Organizations use a variety of mechanisms such as staff development and appraisal schemes, team development and motivational skills to encourage and support improved individual and group performance.

The six mechanisms can be used to identify the way in which local authorities are attempting to manage performance and how that is changing. It may be argued that in some local authorities increased use of planning and control systems has been the focus of change. In many local authorities, and in society generally, the challenge to professionalism may have led to a diminution of its importance as a guarantee of good performance. Market and economic mechanisms which often were significantly lacking are now of increasing importance.

Framework 3: Settings

There are different settings in which performance needs to be considered. Three of these can be immediately identified as:

1 THE GOVERNMENTAL SETTING

The requirement for a local authority to account for its performance to its customers, its citizens, and to central government and its agencies. The accountability requirements are generally specified in law and in regulations which determine in part how a local authority should organize itself, how it should act and what information it should provide. Many local authorities, in pursuit of their governmental role, choose to go beyond the minimum requirements of legislation.

2 THE ORGANIZATIONAL SETTING

The need for a local authority to determine procedures, systems and structures which enable it, firstly, to determine its aims and objectives, set its plans and budgets, and secondly, to control, monitor and review its actions and achievements.

3 THE INDIVIDUAL SETTING

Organizational performance is ultimately dependent on human resources – in terms of action, skills and commitment. Managing the performance of human beings, whether individually or in groups, is in part concerned with the rational procedures of goal setting, planning and reviewing but is also concerned with providing a climate and procedures which encourage and allow them to perform to their full ability and which enable them to extend their capacity to perform.

All three settings are interrelated and integral to the performance of local authorities. The two components of the organizational setting (planning and controlling) are not of great meaning unless they are related closely to the individual setting, while the third setting, institutional accountability, cannot be achieved fully without appropriate procedures for the internal management of performance of the organization and the individuals who work within it.

To these three settings it is necessary to add a fourth consideration – that of the local authority as *community government*. In its role of government of the community or locality the performance of a local authority can be expressed narrowly in terms of its accountability. It can however be expressed more widely in terms of the leadership, support and encouragement it gives to the community. It can also be expressed in terms of the extent to which it successfully interacts with its community and the extent to which it acquires or attracts resources on behalf of its community.

Framework 4: Towards integration

Drawing the various strands together it now becomes possible to develop a more integrated model of how they can consider its management. The model, illustrated in Figure 2.1 has four components:

QUADRANT A – THE GOVERNMENT OF COMMUNITY

▽ Accountability – mechanisms for reporting, informing, and for citizens to express their views and judgements.
▽ Enabling and Interacting – which includes informing citizens in the widest sense, informing itself of community needs and expectations by means of community monitoring and review procedures, acquiring and attracting resources.

In this quadrant the primary focus in terms of performance is on responsiveness, interaction and adaption.

QUADRANT B – THE ACTIVE PRODUCER OF SERVICES

▽ which is concerned with those components of the internal management process for determining strategy and with setting aims, objectives, goals and targets. In this quadrant the primary focus in terms of performance is on direction and the maximization of organizational output.

QUADRANT C – THE WELL-REGULATED BUREAUCRACY

▽ which is concerned with establishing controls, checks and reviews and with procedures for internal auditing and standard setting. In this quadrant the primary focus in terms of performance is on establishing controls to ensure and check that the organization's plans and targets are being achieved in an efficient way.

QUADRANT D – THE ORGANIZATION OF COMMITTED PEOPLE

▽ which is concerned with developing the motivation and commitment of those who work within the local authority. It involves their active participation and involvement in planning and reviewing and in problem-solving. It involves providing opportunities for their training and development, and establishing communication patterns which travel upwards and across the organization, as well as downwards. In this quadrant the primary focus in terms of performance is on maximizing the contribution of all individuals and groups to the local authority by encouraging their personal development and involvement.

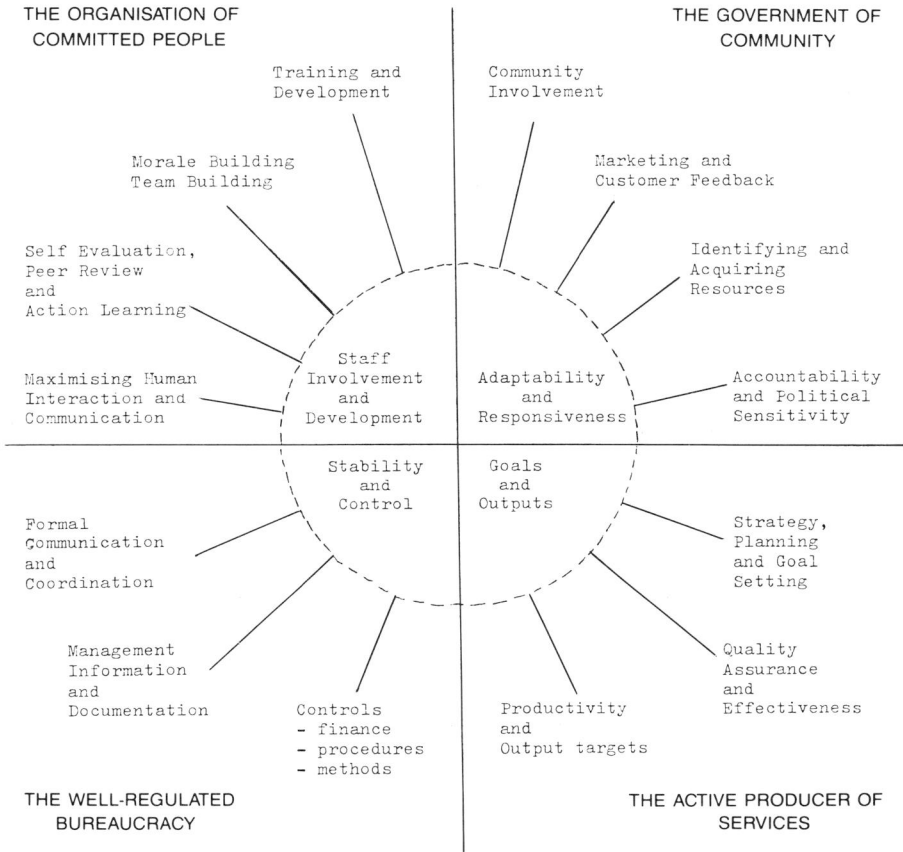

THE ORGANISATION OF
COMMITTED PEOPLE

THE GOVERNMENT OF
COMMUNITY

Training and
Development

Community
Involvement

Morale Building
Team Building

Marketing and
Customer Feedback

Self Evaluation,
Peer Review
and
Action Learning

Identifying and
Acquiring
Resources

Maximising Human
Interaction and
Communication

Staff
Involvement
and
Development

Adaptability
and
Responsiveness

Accountability
and Political
Sensitivity

Stability
and
Control

Goals
and
Outputs

Formal
Communication
and
Coordination

Strategy,
Planning
and Goal
Setting

Management
Information
and
Documentation

Controls
- finance
- procedures
- methods

Productivity
and
Output targets

Quality
Assurance
and
Effectiveness

THE WELL-REGULATED
BUREAUCRACY

THE ACTIVE PRODUCER OF
SERVICES

Figure 2.1 Local Authority Performance – Towards Integration

Implicit in this model of performance is the concept of *balance* between the four quadrants. Performance is a function not only of good planning and target setting, it is also a function of human commitment. Performance is not achieved through tight internal controls *or* responsiveness to the community, it is achieved through *both*. All four quadrants are essential to any local authority which wishes to improve its performance.

In practice at any one moment in time, a local authority is unlikely to have fully achieved that concept of balance. Its political and managerial focus may have led to an emphasis on quadrants B and C at the expense of A and D, or a dominant concern with quadrant A may have arisen without a continuing focus on quadrant C.

Achieving a sense of balance, and having the ability to make adjustments in the light of external and internal pressures, is not easy. It requires constant analysis of the state of the organization and its changing environment. But it is the most important task of managing performance.

Questions

▲ *How much agreement is there in your authority as to the meaning of the terms introduced in the early part of this chapter?*

▲ *How important is the concept of Accountability in Managing Performance?*

▲ *Using Framework 1, can you identify the most important performance problems in your authority?*

▲ *With reference to Framework 4, to what extent does your authority achieve balance between the four quadrants?*

3 Developing a framework for performance management

Outline

In Chapter 2 the key concepts and terminology of performance management were introduced. The purpose of this chapter is to examine how those concepts have been developed in practical terms by individual local authorities with particular attention being given to systems and procedures which aim to provide a clear focus on how the local authority is performing. A number of examples are provided, with no one example being regarded as appropriate for all local authorities, although the examples are grouped in terms of what appears to be a progression over time in the approach and style adopted.

Performance management systems and procedures – some thematic issues

The phrase 'thematic issues' is used to represent a number of key issues and considerations which emerge from the examples which follow later in the chapter. They are all issues which need to be borne in mind by local authorities when they are considering their own approach to performance management. For the sake of clarity the issues are presented as a series of statements opposed, but in practice matters are not so sharply distinguished and they may therefore more properly be regarded as the extreme ends of a continuum.

Issue 1: Total systems v. partial systems

In a few local authorities the approach to managing performance may be described as a 'total systems approach' in so far as they have an overall framework or system of management, which provides a clear focus on performance at all stages of the policy making and management process; which is local authority wide, covering all services and activities; which involves both councillors and officers; and which integrates a number of sub-systems and procedures which in other authorities proceed independently of each other. These systems are therefore 'total' in two fundamental ways:

▽ horizontally, ie. they are corporate
▽ vertically, i.e. they have an influence from the top to bottom of the local authority's organizational structure.

In such authorities the overall system of management provides a clear framework which determines how, when and by whom the inter-related processes of planning, action, monitoring and reviewing are effected. They are the driving forces which both determine and reflect the general values and style of the local authority.

In the majority of local authorities the approach to performance management is more partial, representing only one of several approaches to management with which it has to co-exist and sometimes compete. The impact of such partial approaches is likely to be perceived and experienced quite differently by the various participants in the process of management. For some it will be a critical and major influence on their thoughts and actions, whilst others may be hardly aware of its existence. In some local authorities performance management – particularly as represented by the reporting of performance indicators, the presentation of annual performance reports and the carrying out of ad hoc performance review exercises – gives the appearance of having been 'tacked-on' as an incidental afterthought to the main corporate and departmental management processes.

Issue 2: Top-down v bottom-up approaches

In some local authorities the major impact and intent of performance management flow from a perceived need to 'give direction to' the local authority and to provide procedures which ensure that there are appropriate controls over what is done and achieved. In such authorities the general style or approach adopted tends to be clearly hierarchical (top-down) in nature. It starts with the specification of broad corporate aims and objectives, translating them successively downwards through the organization to the point where individual members of staff have specific objectives and key results areas determined. The downwards specification of direction, objectives and expected results is then matched by an upwards process of monitoring and reviewing.

The hierarchical approach contrasts with that adopted by some local authorities which may be described as bottom-up in that the initial or primary focus on performance is directed at the individual officer or at a cost-centre or service unit level. Such approaches are generally more concerned with generating motivation, enthusiasm and the willingness of individuals and small units to monitor, review and appraise their own performance.

In practice a number of local authorities attempt to adopt an approach which reflects both a top-down and a bottom-up style of management. Clearly any local authority requires a sense of strategy and direction which must be determined at the most senior levels, and clearly it must be able to check whether that sense of strategy and direction is being achieved in practice. But an excessive degree of direction and control can create an environment in which individuals merely seek to conform to what is required of them without contributing to the process of problem-solving and planning in an active way.

Issue 3: Action v. analysis

All approaches to the management of local government are, at the most general level, concerned with action (i.e. specifying what is to be done and ensuring that it is done) and with analysis (i.e. examining the effects and consequences of that action). But a difference can be discerned between those authorities in which the primary concern and orientation appears to be with action and those in which the orientation is more towards analysis. In the former the key words and phrases used which represent the general concern with getting things done are 'action plans', 'key results areas' and 'goals', whereas in the latter the terms 'review', 'evaluation' and 'appraisal' are more commonly found. The difference between the two approaches may also be characterized in negative terms as a style of management and framework of thinking which, in the former case, can become overly concerned with the achievement of short term results (often expressed in terms of meeting increased volume and production targets), or which in the latter case can lead to a form of organizational 'paralysis by analysis' in which the process of implementing the results of analysis is over-shadowed by the process of analysis itself. Achieving a sense of balance is crucial.

Issue 4: Direction and control by councillors v. direction and control by officers

Local authorities differ in the extent to which either councillors or officers are involved in directing and controlling the affairs of the authority. In some local authorities it is quite clearly the councillors who both formulate and specify policies. In others, although councillors in a formal sense decide policies, it is the officers who are more involved in the process of formulating and articulating policy, a process which they undertake on behalf of councillors based on their understanding of the general political purpose and sense of direction. The same is true with regard to monitoring and reviewing the performance of the authority, in which councillors either can become extensively involved by means of detailed reporting and analysis of performance or can undertake only a general overview of these processes which are essentially carried out by officers.

The issue of how a local authority can determine the respective roles of councillors and officers – roles which need to be separate, distinguishable, but complementary – is of vital importance but is beyond the scope of this book. However, it is of significance that in some of those authorities described later in this chapter as having well articulated and 'total' systems and procedures for managing performance, the respective roles of councillors and officers have been clearly defined. Indeed it may be argued that in some cases the very existence of a well articulated and documented process of management acts for councillors as a form of 'quality assurance' that the authority is being well managed in detail by their officers, thereby allowing them to concentrate on matters of more strategic importance and to be much more selective in deciding which detailed aspects of service they need to become involved with.

Issue 5: Continuity v. change – in systems, personnel and political control

It cannot be considered simply a matter of chance that several of the authorities used as examples in this chapter can be described as having a considerable measure of stability and continuity in the performance management systems they have set up, in the personnel at chief and senior officer levels who were responsible for designing, implementing and developing those systems, and in the political control of the authority. It may be argued that a degree of continuity is essential because of the length of time it takes to design and implement such systems, and, more importantly, to change the general culture and style of the authority to one which is more performance conscious. In many cases it appears that the process of change, where it has a real rather than marginal impact on the management of the authority, takes place over a period of years rather than months. Equally important is the process of sustaining such systems (especially in the early period of their implementation when they may be under attack from a variety of stakeholders in the local authority who see their own roles, styles and interests being challenged) and the gradual process of improvement, refinement and development which inevitably must take place. Constant changes of leadership, at councillor and officer levels, appear to militate against the development of corporate systems and procedures which have a real impact on the local authority.

Conversely change of personnel is often a pre-requisite for introducing the drive towards more performance conscious procedures and systems for managing local authorities. In several of the examples, it is quite clear that it is new leaders, at either officer or councillor level, who are the catalysts for major change.

Issue 6: An internal focus v. an external focus

Approaches to performance management may also vary in the extent to which they are predominantly internally focused, in which case they will tend to be more concerned with the efficiency of internal procedures. The mechanisms for setting performance goals and for monitoring and reviewing achievement will also be inward-looking, contained within the local authority or even within separate departments. Those authorities which are more externally focused will tend to be more concerned with the effectiveness of their services, and the mechanisms for goal setting, monitoring and review are more likely to focus on customers and clients.

Managing performance – total systems approaches

One of the main difficulties faced by local authorities in trying to focus more explicitly on managing their performance is their own complex nature. The complexity is reflected in their many differing purposes and objectives, the variety of decision-making and management procedures, the different organizational structures contained within them, and the many differing political, managerial and professional values and ideologies which they represent. The existence of these layers of complexity has led to one analysis of local government which concludes that there have been three particular weaknesses in the traditional way they have been managed:

▽ a lack of overall direction and purpose
▽ a lack of cohesion and co-ordination which results in different parts of the local authority being able to adopt their own goals, expectations and standards of performance
▽ an absence of corporate, and sometimes even departmental management information systems to enable councillors and senior managers to know who is doing what, at what cost and with what effect. As a consequence accountability is weak or even non-existent.

Linked to this kind of analysis was a view that there was a general failure within local authorities to be sufficiently concerned with ensuring that the many complex organizational procedures and structures were properly directed at achieving practical results in terms of delivering services to the community. This critique pointed local authorities towards becoming more action-oriented and maximizing the volume, economy and efficiency of their services.

The final strand of this critique of local government management was directed at the employees of local authorities. If the staff of local authorities (and other public sector organizations) were considered to be relatively unproductive, and lacking both motivation and initiative, it was clearly insufficient simply to blame and castigate them – the reasons for this state of affairs needed to be analysed and the situation rectified. The analysis was not difficult to make. In so far as local authorities were complex organizations, with multiple, detailed controls which constrained individual initiative, it was not surprising that high levels of productivity and motivation were lacking. Indeed, where individual employees were required to work under such constraints it may be argued that it was only the strong sense of professionalism and commitment to public service which existed in most local authorities which ensured that services were produced and delivered.

The impact of the kinds of analysis outlined above was to encourage some local authorities to create a more corporate and integrated approach to managing their performance and to develop what are described here as 'Performance Management Systems'. This term is used in a broader way than it is in some local authorities where it refers only to the process of managing the performance of individual employees. The characteristics of such systems are that they are corporate systems which include the following processes as part of an annual integrated cycle of management:

▽ setting corporate policy and resource aims and guidelines
▽ specifying, within the framework provided by (1) above, a detailed set of plans, budgets, objectives, targets and standards of performance
▽ regularly and systematically reviewing the performance of all services.

Performance Management Systems which have the above three characteristics are described below as Group 1 systems, in so far as they focus primarily on organizational performance; i.e. the procedures for planning, monitoring and reviewing are directed at organizational units responsible for the provision of particular services. They are distinct from Group 2 systems which integrate the procedures for managing organizational performance with those for managing the performance of individuals. The latter therefore have the following additional characteristics:

▽ Procedures and systems for planning, monitoring and appraising the performance of individuals which are integrated with those for managing organizational performance.

Some, though not all Group 2 systems, have a fifth characteristic:

▽ Systems, such as performance related pay, for rewarding individual achievements.

It may be argued that all or most local authorities portray some degree of the first three characteristics as they are fundamental to managing any large organization and are therefore not deserving of a special title such as Performance Management Systems. However, the distinguishing feature of those local authorities used as examples of Performance Management Systems is the *extent* of the impact of the systems on the local authority as a whole. Describing them as corporate means that there is a clear, articulated authority-wide system; that there is a clear corporate role in planning and reviewing performance as well as a service committee and departmental role. It does not mean that they are a corporate overlay of little significance or a system of management which remains driven by semi-autonomous service committees and departments. Describing them as annual integrated systems of management means that they do integrate the otherwise poorly connected procedures for service planning, resource planning and allocation and performance monitoring and review. Their use of objectives, targets and standards is not, as has been the case in some local authorities in the past, an abstract exercise divorced from the realities of everyday management and therefore of little interest or relevance to councillors and officers.

Group 1 systems – managing organizational performance

The local authority which has been most frequently used in recent years as a model of this kind is the London Borough of Bexley and it is this authority, together with Arun District Council, which will be used as the main examples. Before describing the systems adopted by these authorities, it is important to note that while there are some important differences, both have certain general characteristics in common. These are:

▽ both examples draw openly on private sector models of management – it is not irrelevant that their overall approaches are called a 'Business Process' and a 'Business System'.

▽ both systems have had a very real impact on the authority. While elements of both systems bear resemblance to some corporate planning approaches of the 1970's, their real use and impact has been more significant. Whereas a common failing of corporate planning systems was that plans and evaluation were too infrequently translated into action, this is far from the case in Bexley and Arun where the business systems not only provide a political and managerial focus on policy planning, but they also concentrate attention on what has to be done to implement the plans – in both systems it is action planning and the 'Action Plan' which form a central part of the system.

▽ the systems have a real impact also in the sense that the direction and clear expectation of required performance that they produce is not constrained only to senior managers – they have an input well down the organizational hierarchy.

▽ both systems have, in the past, focused primarily on performance in terms of action, economy and efficiency. It may be argued that their concept of performance has been relatively straightforward, eschewing some of the complexities of evaluating outcomes, effectiveness or consumer preferences. This is reflected in the kind of performance indicators and targets used in both authorities which reflected a dominant concern with volume, speed, economy and efficiency of activities. Pollitt (1986) has estimated that approximately 75% of Bexley's performance measures related to economy and efficiency, while only 1% related to effectiveness. However, as John Midgely (1986), the Chief Executive of Arun has demonstrated, the approach adopted in Arun has achieved considerable benefits over several years by increasing the volume of services provided within a standstill budget, and it may be argued that this initial focus on increasing volume and efficiency can be seen in historical terms as an appropriate and necessary development. Both authorities in recent years have amended and developed their approaches to provide a greater concern with managerial and service effectiveness.

▽ although, as has already been stated, both systems require the close involvement of all councillors and officers, it is the Chief Executives and their staff who perform a key role in managing the process. Both approaches produce a strong sense of centralized direction and control.

▽ from a councillor's perspective both approaches provide a clear framework and discipline for corporate policy-making, for service and resource planning and for monitoring and reviewing performance. In so doing, they generate more detailed information about planned and actual performance than is available in the majority of local authorities. There is therefore the potential danger that councillors may become submerged in that detail; but equally, it may be argued that councillors can use the business approach more as an instrument of quality assurance – that is, a visible procedural assurance that the authority is being well managed by its officers – than as an instrument by which they try to effect detailed control of the authority's operations.

Example 1: London Borough of Bexley

The development of the Business Process started in 1974 following the election of a new political administration, the aim of which was to make the local authority more efficient and effective and to reduce the volume of expenditure. The reorganizations and reforms which were implemented over the next few years were based on an analysis which suggested that corporate control of four key areas of decision making needed to be established:

▽ Control of Forward Planning – Policy selection, establishing work targets and information systems which assist in the resource allocation process.
▽ Control of Current Operations – Systematically monitoring actual performance against work targets, comparing costs to achievement.
▽ Control of Resources – Managing key resources of Finance, Personnel and Land in a way that provides vital information to respond to changing economic conditions.
▽ Control of the Organization – Ensuring the necessary functions are present, sensibly grouped, well co-ordinated, with good systems of communication. (Source: Burgess 1983)

The process of change which followed was carried out in two ways. First there was a structural reorganization resulting in the creation of four Service Directorates and three Support Directorates (later reduced to two) and a Management Board consisting of the Chief Executive and Directors. The committee structure was also reorganized so that it corresponded more closely to the officer structure and to the Business Process. The second, and in this context more important, aspect of change, was the design and implementation of the Business Process itself. The Process may be represented in two parts – the policy and resource planning process which is concerned with the annual review and updating of the three year Policy and Resource Plan (see Figure 3.1) and second, the annual process of implementing that plan and monitoring and reviewing performance (see Figure 3.2). The Process is cyclical in nature, working to a tightly ordered programme and it creates a number of key documents:

BOROUGH TRENDS REPORT (ANNUAL)

The document provides a general backcloth to policy making and resource allocation and provides information about the Borough in terms of trends and changes in the population, social groups, economic activity and the physical environment. Its purpose is to highlight changing needs and priorities so that resources can be reallocated accordingly.

3-YEAR CENTRAL POLICY AND RESOURCE PLAN (ANNUAL)

The plan brings together the agreed service development proposals for a 3-year period with the 1st year acting as the starting point for the annual revenue and manpower budgets and the capital programme.

ACTION PLAN (ANNUAL)

From the point of view of managing performance, the creation of this document is of key importance and is a distinctive feature of Bexley's

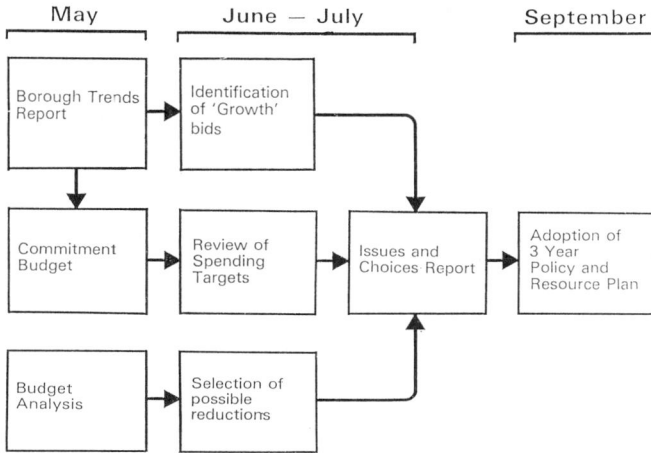

Figure 3.1 Bexley London Borough – Business Process (Stage I)

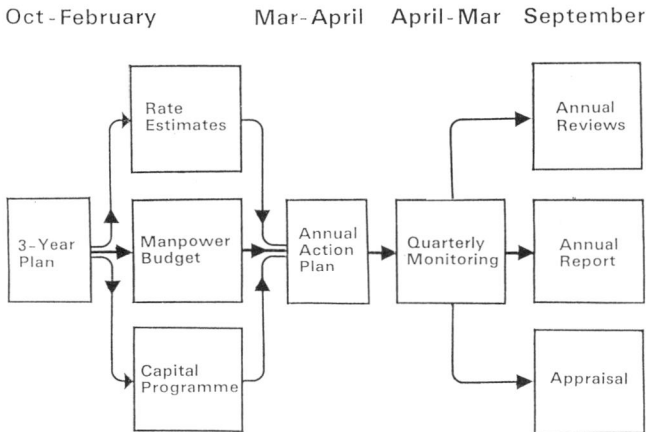

Figure 3.2 Bexley London Borough – Business Process (Stage II)

system. It is based on Year 1 of the Central Policy and Resource Plan and contains, on a committee basis, the following information:

▽ policy objectives to be achieved or tackled during the year. The objectives are stated at a level of considerable detail.

▽ timetables for major items to be presented to Committees.

▽ performance standards and targets for every department (an example of which is given in Figure 3.3). It is the use of these standards and targets which have caused considerable interest in other local authorities, although they have also been subjected to some criticism. While they are of considerable importance in so far as officers are keenly aware of them, their place in the overall process can be overstated. They constitute only one part of an overall process which emphasises planning and reviewing as well as the monitoring of performance against the targets and standards.

(1) **TOWN PLANNING DEPARTMENT**		*Anticipated Workload*	*Target Performance*
(i)	Planning applications		
	(a) Committee applications	600	85% in 13 weeks
	(b) Delegated applications	2,000	100% in 13 weeks
	(c) Overall total	2,600	96% in 13 weeks
	(d) Estimated fee income	£125,000	
(ii)	Appeals	90	100% of written representation statements within 28 days of the starting date 100% of Public Inquiry written (Rule 6) statements within 6 weeks of the relevant date
(iii)	Enforcements	600	Respond to 100% in 3 weeks. Resolve 50% in 8 weeks. Resolve 75% in 12 weeks.
(iv)	Building Regulations		
	(a) Initial applications	2,000	) 100% within) the
	(b) Resubmitted applications and amended plans	1,400	) prescribed) period.
	(c) Building notices	750	
	(d) Inspections – notifiable	25,000	100% in 24 hours.
	(e) Estimated fee income	£300,000	
(v)	House Renovation Grants		
	(a) Applications – Part 1 Carry out survey and produce schedule of works	465	70% in 4 weeks 90% in 8 weeks
	(b) Applications – Part 2 Check estimate and return to Housing Department	310	90% in 2 weeks 100% in 4 weeks
	(c) Payment inspections	450	60% in 2 weeks 90% in 4 weeks
(vi)	Land Charges Searches	12,000	90% in 4 days 100% in 8 days

Figure 3.3 Example of Bexley's Performance Standards and Targets. (Bexley London Borough 'Action Plan 1989/90')

QUARTERLY MONITORING REPORTS

These reports monitor progress and performance and are reported to committees at three levels:

▽ Chief Officers submit Quarterly Operation Reports to their sub-committees.
▽ these reports are then summarized in a report by the relevant Director to Strategic Committees.
▽ the Chief Executive then reports to Policy and Resources Committee on behalf of the Management Board.

The reports provide current information on:

▽ service delivery and achievement against targets
▽ departmental workloads
▽ public demand for services
▽ other key service indicators of effectiveness
▽ resource utilization and expenditure projections.

ANNUAL SERVICE REVIEWS

At the end of each year, a review of performance is provided for each strategic committee. The report brings together the information contained in the previous quarterly reports. The review compares performance against plans and targets for the year as well as with previous years and with other authorities.

As can be seen from the above outline, the Business Process generates a considerable amount of information which is used to support four key areas of management:

▼ Policy planning
▼ Policy formulation and resource allocation
▼ Policy implementation and target setting
▼ Performance monitoring and review.

It is a comprehensive system in that it covers all services. That part of it which relates to the annual action planning process is essentially a management information system which enables the authority to focus on the following key decision areas:

▼ what SERVICES are to be provided?
▼ at what VOLUME?
▼ at what COST?
▼ at what STANDARD of performance?

It does not as a matter of course, deal with questions such as:

▼ how are services to be provided?
▼ what alternative ways of achieving policies exist?

Questions such as these are addressed by means of annual programmes of efficiency and effectiveness studies which provide a more detailed analysis and review of particular services and areas of expenditure. (Source: Burgess 1983)

Example 2: Arun District Council

The reorganizations and reforms of Arun's 'Corporate Business System' were not dissimilar to those of Bexley's. The combination of a large Conservative majority in the 1983 elections, a new political leadership requiring a greater sense of purpose and direction in the authority, and the arrival of a new Chief Executive, all combined to create the conditions for a radical appraisal of management structures and systems which enabled the Chief Executive to develop a strategic framework for change which incorporated three types of development: Policy development, Organisation development and System and Processes development.

Drawing on the Chief Executive's own analysis of the period (Midgley 1986), the developments may be summarized as follows. *Policy developments* were directed at three key issues:

▽ amalgamation of individual services into eight programme areas as a basis for rationalising services. Each programme area was covered by a statement of key aims and priorities for the following four years. The original document containing these statements, 'The Next Four Years – Arun's Aims and Strategies' was a key expression of political aims, being primarily based on the manifesto, and the four years it covered corresponded to the political administration's term of office.

▽ the adoption of a more outward-looking interest and involvement in those county, regional and national affairs which affected the authority. This was achieved by means of closer and more regular contact with a wide range of public and private institutions.

▽ a more strategic approach to resource management in order to maximize the benefits gained from available resources. This included both a strategic approach to generating additional financial resources and a wide ranging and tight control of existing resources by means of a strong emphasis on economy and efficiency.

Organizational development was achieved by means of a series of changes to political roles, committee organization, departmental organization, operational procedures, and the expansion of staff training and development activities. The essential aim of these developments was to achieve much greater corporate direction and control – at both councillor and officer levels.

Systems and Processes development concentrated on establishing an annual corporate business system which would emphasize political direction and review of achievements. The system adopted is shown in Figure 3.4 and requires some interpretation.

First the words on the left side of the diagram are important because they represent the six stages of the framework provided by the business system and may be used to describe it:

▽ *Direction.* This part of the system is concerned with establishing the main direction of the local authority over a four year period – this part of the system therefore lies outside the annual cycle of activities.

▽ *Planning.* The process of annually translating the four year strategy into a set of more specific policies with a statement of outline resource

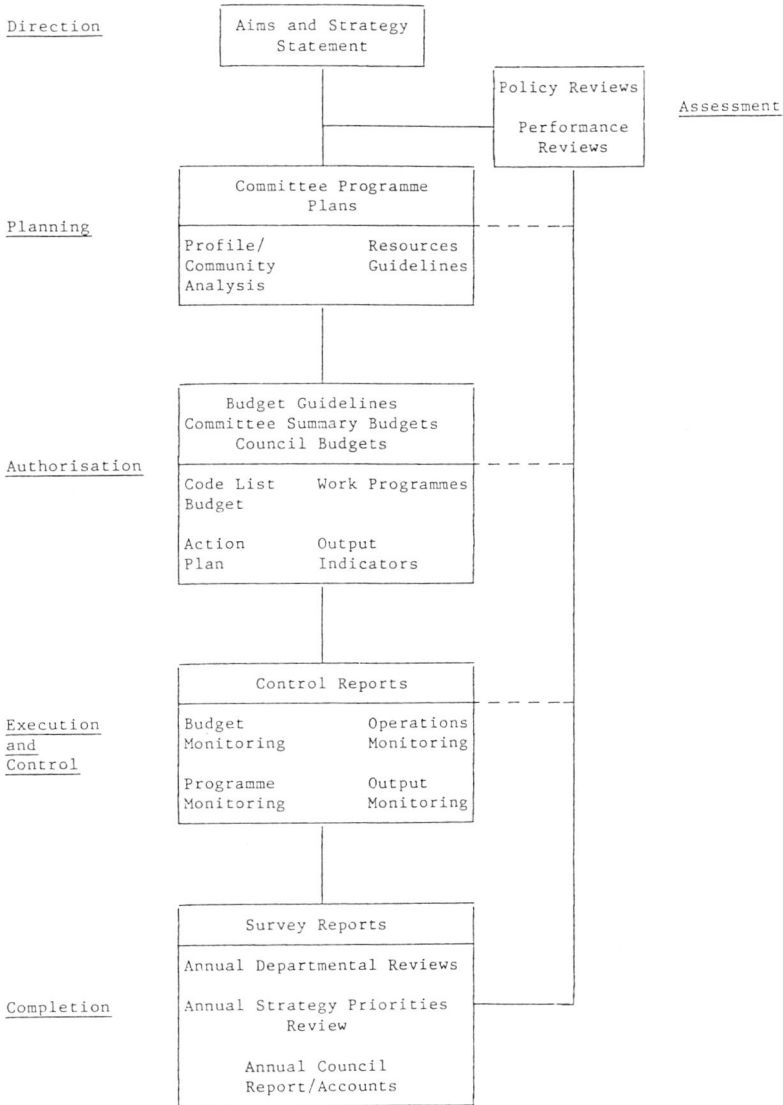

```
Direction          ┌─────────────────────┐
                   │  Aims and Strategy  │
                   │     Statement       │
                   └─────────────────────┘          ┌──────────────────┐
                              │                      │ Policy Reviews   │   Assessment
                              │                      │                  │
                              │                      │ Performance      │
                              │                      │ Reviews          │
                   ┌─────────────────────┐           └──────────────────┘
                   │ Committee Programme  │
Planning           │      Plans          │
                   ├─────────────────────┤ ─ ─ ─ ─
                   │ Profile/    Resources│
                   │ Community   Guidelines│
                   │ Analysis            │
                   └─────────────────────┘

                   ┌─────────────────────┐
                   │   Budget Guidelines  │
                   │ Committee Summary Budgets│
                   │    Council Budgets   │
Authorisation      ├─────────────────────┤ ─ ─ ─ ─
                   │ Code List   Work Programmes│
                   │ Budget              │
                   │                     │
                   │ Action      Output  │
                   │ Plan        Indicators│
                   └─────────────────────┘

                   ┌─────────────────────┐
                   │   Control Reports    │
Execution          ├─────────────────────┤ ─ ─ ─ ─
and                │ Budget      Operations│
Control            │ Monitoring  Monitoring│
                   │                     │
                   │ Programme   Output  │
                   │ Monitoring  Monitoring│
                   └─────────────────────┘

                   ┌─────────────────────┐
                   │   Survey Reports     │
                   ├─────────────────────┤
                   │ Annual Departmental Reviews│
                   │                     │
Completion         │ Annual Strategy Priorities│
                   │      Review         │
                   │                     │
                   │ Annual Council      │
                   │ Report/Accounts     │
                   └─────────────────────┘
```

Figure 3.4 Arun's Corporate Business System Arun District Council 'Strategy Papers and Programme Plans 1987 – 1991

requirements which are presented in Service Plans for each committee. These are also based on a profile and analysis of the community and on a resources review and set of resource guidelines.

▽ *Authorization.* The process of translating service plans into budgets to authorize expenditure and into a detailed work programme which is presented in a corporate Annual Action Plan, which identifies specific objectives and key tasks and a set of associated performance measures.

▽ *Execution and Control.* The process of executive action and the controlling of that action by means of regular monitoring of progress and performance against budgets and action plans. Operational reports are submitted to each cycle of programme committees based on a corporate information system, which provides data on budget variances, performance and progress against targets and a commentary on any special areas of work or projects. In addition, a Performance Review Sub-Committee also receives corporate summaries.

▽ *Completion.* The process of annually reviewing and reporting on performance against plans. The process is conducted at departmental/programme committee level and, perhaps more importantly, corporately by the Policy and Resources Committee which considers the strategic implications of the past year's performance for the next year's annual business process.

▽ *Assessment.* This final stage of the system is in reality a continuous programme of policy and performance reviews (with the emphasis on efficiency) carried out primarily by the Performance Review Sub-Committee. The identification of issues for assessment arises partly internally, from the business system itself, and partly externally, from, for example, the annual audit management letter.

SUMMARIZING: THE 'BUSINESS' APPROACH

The 'Business' approaches adopted in Arun and Bexley in the 1980's had many similar characteristics which make them distinctive. Principal amongst these were:

▽ the degree of corporate direction – expressed through a highly articulated medium-term and annual planning process
▽ the degree of corporate control – expressed through the availability of extensive information on plans, programmes and performance
▽ the exphasis on action and achievement
▽ the importance given to performance measures, targets and standards.
▽ the emphasis given to a continuous process of evaluation and review
▽ the apparent emphasis on the volume, efficiency and economy of services.

Example 3: Chesterfield Borough Council

A not dissimilar but less centralized process is that adopted by Chesterfield, which they call a Corporate Planning System. The process does not involve as many plans and reports as Arun and Bexley, the main document being an annual Corporate Plan which draws together the following information:

▽   A Vision Statement setting out the Council's overall aims and its values and characteristics.
▽   Background Information which includes a borough profile and information about the structure and staffing of the Council.
▽   Key Issues. Each year the Council identifies a limited number of key issues or priorities for the coming year. (six key issues were identified for 1989/90 and five for 1990/91). These are expressed either as major tasks (e.g. to respond effectively to competitive tendering) or as major reviews (e.g. to review policies and practices for the Environment and to draw up an Environmental Charter).
▽   Policy Review Areas. Fundamental to the corporate planning system is a continuous process of performance review, one part of which is the identification each year of a number of policy reviews. In each corporate plan, the issues for review in the coming year are identified and brief information provided on those reviews completed in the last year or still in progress. The reviews tend to be more concerned with issues of effectiveness than with economy and efficiency.
▽   Financial Information, giving an overall view of the Council's financial position.
▽   The Committee Section, which forms the largest part of the corporate plan, is a detailed statement on a committee-by-committee basis of policies, budgets and performance targets and measures.

The Committee Section contains the following information:

▽   Council-wide basis – statement of general policies.
▽   Committee basis. For each of the six main committees of the Council a statement is given of the key issues for the coming year. Where relevant, these are drawn from the corporate key issues (see above) which are supplemented by issues which are determined by each committee. The number of key issues tends to vary between two and five per committee. A summary of the Revenue Budget and Capital Programme under the control of each committee is also provided.
▽   Programme Area basis. The responsibilities of each committee are broken down into programme areas, which are reported on using the following format:
1 Overall objective of area.
2 Statutory Powers relevant to the area.
3 Policies – a statement of the main agreed policies covering the programme areas (which are stated as more detailed objectives).
4 Current Position – a brief, selective statement of major current issues and activities.
5 Performance Review – a statement of specific targets to measure performance against which is reported to committees on a half-yearly basis. The nature of the targets is extremely variable – indeed the Council acknowledges the difficulty of identifying meaningful and measurable targets for some areas of activities, but expresses its determination to do so wherever possible. The targets include:

     – volume and costs of individual activities.
     – project/activity/task completion targets.
     – cost comparisons with the private sector.
     – production of reports on specific issues.
     – speed/timeliness of council response.
     – workload rates and measures.
     – achievement targets in relation to demand/needs.
6 Revenue Estimates – a statement of revenue estimates for the year expressed on a cost centre basis (the number of which varies between 1 and 10 per programme area).

The importance placed on the performance review function within the corporate planning process is expressed in the Leader of the Council's introduction to the 1989/90 Corporate Plan:

> The Corporate Plan will remain a live and working feature of the Council's democratic processes only as long as there is an effective performance review mechanism. This affords Members the opportunity to challenge existing policies and also to take a critical look at non-achievements, as well as acknowledging achievements, in order to decide whether changes need to be made in terms of both effectiveness and efficiency. Although it needs to be continuously developed, the reporting process now established, encompassing The Annual Report, the Review of Policy Areas and regular Performance Review reporting, affords Members this opportunity to review the Council's overall performance in providing the public with the services it needs.

The importance of Chesterfield's approach is:

▽ performance review is conceived as an integral and continuous part of the management process
▽ there is an emphasis both on the review of policy effectiveness (Policy Reviews) and on the monitoring and review of implementation (Performance targets and monitoring)
▽ the system is perceived by the authority as being evolutionary rather than static.

Group 2 systems – integrating organizational and individual performance

The distinguishing feature of these systems is the extent to which they consciously and systematically attempt to translate the procedures for planning, monitoring and reviewing performance down to the level of the individual member of staff, thereby integrating the management of organizational performance with that of individual performance. Within these systems there is an explicit recognition that:

▽ the performance of the local authority is ultimately dependent on the performance of each individual member of its staff
▽ each member of staff must be clearly and individually accountable for what he/she does and achieves
▽ the discipline of regularly setting objectives and work plans, of monitor-

ing and reviewing or appraising performance, should be applied individually as well as organizationally

▽   individuals are more likely to work productively and effectively when they can place their own activities within a clear framework of broader policies, goals and targets

▽   individuals are more likely to be motivated when they are personally involved in determining their objectives, goals and targets of performance.

The distinction between Group 1 and 2 systems is not an absolute one – it is one of degree. It reflects the relative focus of the corporate management process on organizational, as distinct from individual, performance and the extent to which the procedures for managing both are formally integrated. It should not therefore be concluded that those authorities used as examples of Group 1 systems do not have procedures, both corporate and departmental, for managing individuals, for they do. Those procedures have not however formed the primary focus in creating and developing the corporate or business process. It is also important to note that the three examples provided of Group 1 systems are all now involved in a process of significant change and development and the description provided of them is inevitably historical in nature. Bexley, for example, has recently undertaken two significant changes both of which are designed to improve the integration of procedures for managing individual and organizational performance, and it is for this reason that it is also used as an emerging example of Group 2 systems.

Example 1: London Borough of Bexley

The first recent development to the Business Process has been the introduction of directorate Work Plans, the major purpose of which is to clarify individual responsibility for each task specified in the Action Plan. It is an elaboration of the action planning process representing a shift from organizational to individual performance. The second change relates to the development of an existing performance appraisal system, in order to make it less focused on the accomplishment of short-term tasks and more related to the broader concept of managerial effectiveness.

Example 2: Cambridgeshire County Council

Cambridgeshire was one of the first local authorities to create a corporate system which integrated individual and organizational performances, based on a hierarchy of planning processes. At the corporate level, the basis of planning is provided by a three-year medium-term planning system in which the plan is rolled forward each year and forms the basis of the annual budgeting exercise and the preparation of service plans for each department. The service plans set out the strategic direction for departmental development, one-year objectives and targets and a three-year strategy based on agreed policies. The medium-term and service planning processes form a 'top-down' approach to planning:

they set the parameters for individual departments and provide essential political guidance from the executive committees of the County Council (Cambridgeshire County Council: Social Services Planning Manual 1988)

This 'top-down' approach is complemented by a 'bottom-up' approach which, within the Social Services Department, consists of a hierarchy of unit, locality and divisional plans each of which contain annual objectives which then form the basis for determining the goals for individual members of staff within an equally well-defined process of performance appraisal.

Example 3: The Royal Borough of Windsor and Maidenhead

Windsor and Maidenhead describe their Performance Management Programme as 'a structured but flexible approach to improving the performance of individual members of staff, of sections, divisions, departments and of the organization as a whole.' Each department operates a planning process, illustrated in Figure 3.5, which provides the information needed for corporate management purposes. Within the departmental process, there is a clear recognition of the importance of effective individual performance, and this is reflected in the development of what is essentially a 'bottom-up' approach based on five primary techniques:

∇   function and target setting
∇   pyramid performance monitoring – which begins at section level and results in the specification of key tasks for the department and a set

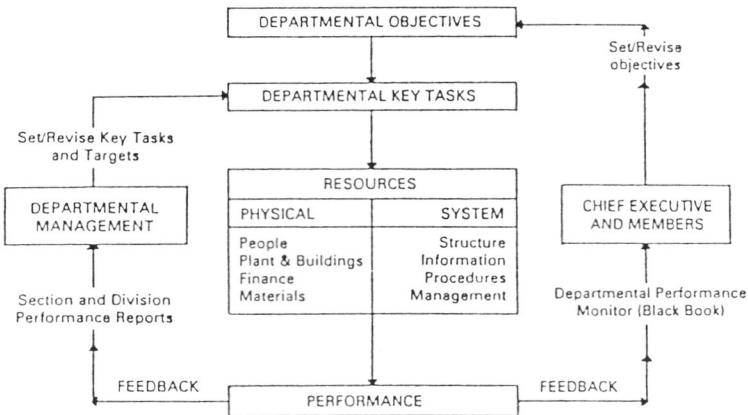

Figure 3.5 Windsor and Maidenhead's Performance Management Programme – a model of the departmental process.
(Royal Borough of Windsor and Maidenhead 'Performance Management')

of performance indicators for monitoring the key tasks (The Black Book)

▽ structure and communications – which focuses on teamwork and team development and the establishment of clear lines of communication

▽ staff development and appraisal – involving annual appraisal of all staff including chief officers

▽ management information – the design of new management information systems to support the process.

Although the previous three examples have many differences, they each represent the increasing recognition in local government that procedures for planning and reviewing organizational performance will not be effective unless closely linked with procedures for managing staff at all levels. In some local authorities, the emphasis is very much on individual account-ability, while in others there is an equal emphasis on team-work. In both cases, however, the systems created aim to ensure that individual objectives and aspirations are linked as closely as possible to those of the organization.

Other approaches

Many other authorities are attempting to develop more integrated approaches to performance management. The Metropolitan Borough of Rochdale is implementing a performance review system, which is intended to operate at three levels. The Macro level consists of a process of setting departmental objectives and identifying performance measures, while the Intermediate level comprises a co-ordinated programme of reviews, examining specific activities in depth with a view to improving quality and cost effectiveness. The Micro level rests on the belief that

a complete performance review system should include ways of unlock-ing the potential drive, energy and enthusiasm of our workforce along with opportunities for individual staff development. Possible methods include job consultation/staff development, and practical and workable suggestion schemes.
(Metro Rochdale, Chief Executive and Town Clerk's Department – Report on Performance Review for Metro Rochdale, October 1988)

Buckinghamshire County Council is introducing a performance manage-ment scheme which, at the organizational level, results in the production of annual action plans for each committee containing key tasks and objec-tives. The action plans form the basis of the annual process of setting key objectives and priority tasks for managers within departments which is undertaken as part of an annual performance appraisal process.

Group 3 systems – the contracting authority

There are now a number of local authorities who have begun to develop an internal contract culture, which may be seen as an important mechanism for managing performance. While approaches to contract management cannot be described as systems in quite the same sense as those described in some of the previous examples, they nonetheless are beginning to exert a powerful influence on the way performance is managed and defined. Lincolnshire County Council is an example of an authority which has adopted this approach, by extending the principles of competition well beyond those activities subject to compulsory competitive tendering. The services involved are printing, computing, materials testing, civil engineering design, legal services, vehicle hire, personnel, property and finance. The precise contractual arrangements for each service vary, in many cases being based on service level agreements.

There are two elements to the contract culture, which are of fundamental importance to the way in which performance is managed. First, it requires the specification of services in precise volume, quality and cost terms, to an extent which rarely occurs, and is probably resisted, when services are provided on an in-house basis. Secondly, it requires the separation of roles within the authority, which may be expressed basically in terms of a client-contractor split. The consequence of creating these organizationally distinctive roles is to change the basis of management from what was essentially either a command culture or a concensus and bargaining culture to one of a contract culture.

The gradual increase in the use of service level agreements by central departments, such as accountancy, legal and personnel services has also had an impact in requiring those departments to define more clearly their role, in the sense of distinguishing between those activities which are essentially support services to other departments and their necessary corporate activities, involving strategic and resource planning and control. Service level agreements have also had the effect of causing greater attention and analysis to be given to those central departments, which in some local authorities may have been least directly affected by previous economy and efficiency programmes. Their benefits therefore lie as much in requiring central departments to be generally more performance conscious, as they do in reducing the extent of overheads paid by service departments.

It is as yet too early to evaluate the benefits of a more widespread contract culture. There are many evident benefits arising from the sharpening up of management practices, the need to be performance conscious and the development of management information systems. There is, however, the potential danger that contracts and service level agreements can produce levels of inflexibility and competitiveness which will not be ultimately beneficial for all types of service. A contractual basis for managing services does, however, represent a dramatic change in the nature of public service management.

4 Measuring performance

Outline

The essential message of this chapter is that performance measurement is necessary and important. Without it managers are less able to manage effectively and accountability is less easily achieved. Attitudes towards performance measurement vary considerably – fascination, fear and indifference are all frequently expressed. It creates strong feelings which are partly concerned with how measures are used and by whom they are used, and partly concerned with the complexities of specifying and measuring performance.

The purpose of this chapter is to examine some of the psychological barriers and methodological complexities which surround performance measurement and to identify some practical approaches to its use.

Just four questions lie at the heart of using performance measures successfully. They are:

▽ Why do you want to measure? – What are the purposes of measurement?
▽ Who are the measures for? – Who is meant to use them?
▽ What do you want to measure? – What characteristics of performance are important?
▽ How are you going to measure? – What methods should be used for collecting, analysing and presenting data?

A position statement

Performance measurement has been the subject of considerable debate for a number of years, but it is mainly in the last decade that significant developments in its practical application have been made. The Government, in pursuit of its objective of making the public sector more dynamically performance-orientated, has played a critical role in some of these developments. Within the civil service one can point to a number of initiatives which have had at their heart the creation of better information about performance. These include examples such as MINIS (Management Information for Ministers System); ARM (Activity and Resource Management System), and most importantly, FMI (Financial Management Initiative). At the local government level its initiatives have included the requirement to publish Annual Reports and Accounts, the requirement to publish specific information about particular services such as schools and housing management, the introduction of compulsory competitive tendering (thereby forcing local authorities to consider how they can measure the performance of their contractors), and the creation of the Audit Commission.

At the same time, local authorities have themselves successfully implemented and utilized performance measures to a greater extent than ever before, as many of the examples provided in the previous chapter amply illustrate. Many of those developments have been very much local developments, stimulated and implemented by the officers and councillors in individual local authorities and are not simply responses to the persuasion, threats or requirements of central government. In those authorities at least, performance measurement has played a key part in creating a more performance-conscious climate.

The new orthodoxy – the Audit Commission's three E's

In order to measure performance it is clearly necessary to be able to define what is meant by performance. But the 'performance' of a local authority, or even of a single service, is a complex and multi-faceted concept and the inability to define or describe it has in the past been one of the key blockages to the development of measures. In addition, technical problems relating to the validity, reliability and availability of certain kinds of data needed for performance measurement have been seen as reasons for caution.

What was required was a methodology or framework for describing performance, and this was provided for local authorities by the Audit Commission by their promotion and definition of the three E's. Performance was defined as having three aspects – Economy, Efficiency and Effectiveness. These were not new concepts, but their real value lay not in the fact that they broke new analytical ground but in the fact that the Audit Commission, by means of a largely successful combination of forcefulness, dynamism, persuasion and the use of legal powers, was able to give them a primacy and importance which they had not attained before. Local authorities were made aware that they were to be judged, and should judge themselves, in terms of Economy, Efficiency and Effectiveness. Within local authorities the views of the Audit Commission were more eagerly accepted by those officers and councillors who saw their role primarily in terms of resource management and control, but perhaps less eagerly by those who saw themselves as service providers.

The Audit Commission has remained a strong advocate of performance measurement and has provided local authorities with an almost continuous stream of advice and information. It has significantly developed the use of inter-authority comparisons by means of its use of the families (or clusters) of local authorities having similar demographic and socio-economic characteristics which are used to compile 'Audit Profiles' for individual authorities. The fact that this important and useful body of work has not been universally well received can be ascribed partly to the simple fact that the Commission is perceived as an agent of central government policy. It can also be ascribed to the fact that, in presenting the case for performance measurement, its earlier publications tended to err on the side of ignoring the problems and pitfalls of measurement. In particular, the Commission, until quite recently, focused its attentions to a great extent on the measurement of efficiency and economy with little apparent regard for effectiveness. In defence of the Audit Commission (if it needs defending!) it was clearly tactically quite correct initially to concentrate on issues which were more immediately measurable, and where it could therefore have a more immediate impact.

Some problems and pitfalls

Despite the interests and developments which have taken place, and the important role of the three E's in defining performance, local authorities have experienced problems in identifying and using performance measures and many of them consider that they have a very incomplete and inadequate set of measures. In part this may be due to an unrealistic expectation that, somewhere, the perfect set of performance measures was waiting to be discovered. While that was clearly unrealistic, many of the concerns expressed by councillors and officers are relevant and deserve attention. They can be grouped into five main categories.

1 DEFINITIONAL PROBLEMS

Although the words 'economy', 'efficiency' and 'effectiveness' are frequently used in everyday language in all sorts of contexts, they are in fact quite difficult to define in a way which meets with common understanding and which ensures that distinct aspects of performance are being measured. The problem of achieving common understanding can be illustrated from evidence obtained in training situations. When officers and councillors who claim they have heard of and know about the three E's have been asked to define them, they have sometimes produced very different definitions. Even after having the Audit Commissions's definitions presented to them, followed by explanations and discussion, they have found it difficult to identify corectly performance measures of economy or efficiency or effectiveness.

This evidence should not be read as a criticism of the knowledge or intellectual capacity of those involved. Rather the opposite – a sympathetic concern for their predicament is more appropriate. What it does illustrate is that the words are used in different ways by different people. The Audit Commission's use of the word 'Economy' does not equate well with its variety of meanings in common parlance and the use of the derivatives 'economist', 'economic' and 'economical' only further complicate matters. The definition of the second 'E', Efficiency, appears on the face of it to be practical and straightforward, but it is very different to an economist's use of the term.

The argument can be extended to the question of whether the three E's are clearly distinguishable from each other. Their definitions do distinguish them, but when local authorities try to derive performance measures from them problems begin to arise. Take the following simple example from the Library Service.

'The time taken to meet requests for books which are not on the shelves'.

In one sense it is an indicator of the efficiency of a library system in identifying where a book is, moving it from one location to another and informing the reader that it is then available. But for the reader the speed with which requests are met may be a key element in the way the service is valued – it is therefore for the reader an indicator of service effectiveness. While there is nothing fundamentally incorrect about using a single measure to illustrate different aspects of performance, it does tend to add to confusion and raise doubts about the validity of the concepts.

'Linguistic pedantry' might well be one response to the preceding points, but it is more than that. If, in promoting performance-oriented management, words and concepts are used which are either not clear or not meaningful, then they cannot be expected to have any strong influence on those people whose actions they are intended to influence.

Nor, must it be said, do those who may be presumed to be experts necessarily create clarity. Readers of this book will no doubt have found many points of terminological dispute. Similarly in an otherwise excellent introduction to performance measurement by Jackson and Palmer (1989), doubts and confusion only arise when specific examples of economy and efficiency are put forward to demonstrate the concepts.

2 DATA AVAILABILITY

Performance measurement is dependent, in a technical sense, on the availability of appropriate data on which the measures can be based and on the capability of the local authority to handle that data in an efficient way. The kind of data which is most readily available in most local authorities relates to their own internal production processes. There is plenty of available data about resources and about the quantity of service provided. There is much less data available about the quality of service and its effects on consumers and the public generally. This has resulted in the derivation of many measures of Economy and Efficiency but relatively fewer measures of Effectiveness. In recent years, local authorities have been much more purposeful in their collection of externally generated information through the use of consumer surveys, market research and complaints analysis.

The development of performance measurement has also been handicapped by the lack of computerized information systems which make the manipulation and analysis of large volumes of data possible. The increased availability of desk-top computers with sophisticated software packages for analysing and presenting data have now made the increased use of performance measures a greater practical possibility, for the investment in such systems need not be large. Arun District Council, for example, handles the performance measures in its Business System with one micro-computer using a system developed in Arun – Services Automated Monitoring Information (SAMI). In other authorities the ability to link departmentally-held information bases with those on the authority's mainframe create many more opportunities for developing relevant performance information.

3 OWNERSHIP PROBLEMS

Rightly or wrongly, there is a perception that the concepts and words of the three E's belong to accountants and auditors, and this is compounded by the way their practical implementation has resulted in an almost exclusive focus on costs and volumes of service. Such perceptions give rise to considerable concern, if not outright antagonism, from other participants in the management and provision of services, and these are well illustrated in publications such as 'Whose value? Whose Money?', by Kline and Mallaber. For example:

'The value of local government is increasingly judged in accountancy terms'.

'Accounting techniques cannot measure the output of public services'.

'The accountancy obsession with measurement misses the whole point of many public services. In caring services, it is not always possible to measure everything which counts'.

'Critics within the accountancy profession point out that the accountants professional training does not equip him or her to make what will inevitably be political judgments'.

While such criticisms may be considered valid, they are also unfortunate in that they represent a blockage to the further development not just of performance measures, but to the whole process of creating greater clarity and analysis in local authority management.

The problem is clearly in part about the relative power of various groups and individuals inside (and outside) local government to define how performance is to be judged and to determine which precise criteria and measures will be used. But shifts in power are almost inevitable if local authorities are to respond positively to the widespread and increasing criticisms of their performance expressed by many different groups in society.

If the different participants, or 'stakeholders' in the local government system are to be persuaded to be more performance-conscious, then the question of language (and the concepts which underlie its use) is important. There are many competing languages in local government – the language of party politics, of community action, of accountancy and financial management, of educationalists, engineers, social workers and other professions. The aims and plans of local authorities are expressed in a mixture of these languages and it is probably essential that this should be so if they are to be meaningful to the variety of stakeholders who are expected to contribute to their accomplishment. If 'performance' is expressed only in the language of one set of stakeholders it is less likely to be accepted as a valuable and valid means of guiding actions and decisions.

Concepts of power and the notion of stakeholders have another dimension when applied to performance measurement. The use of performance measures to monitor and review performance is undertaken by a range of groups and individuals both inside the local authority (for example in the case of education it may be head-teachers and governors, education committees and sub-committees, education officers, LEA inspectors, treasurers, auditors, etc.) and outside the authority (e.g. H.M. Inspectors, the Audit Commission, external auditors, parents and pupils). Their definitions of performance, the characteristics of performance on which they focus and the criteria they use may be quite different and sometimes contradictory – as will be their conclusions. When, as is often the case, there is no mechanism for integrating the different perceptions, a situation is created which becomes a breeding ground for prolonged debate and discussion but little activity or decision. The situation is exacerbated when decisions about financial management lie with one group, who are then perceived to have an interest only in economy and efficiency, while service managers focus their concern on questions of effectiveness. The implementation of schemes of devolved management, in so far as they successfully integrate responsibility for resource utilization with the production of services, should go some way to overcoming this particular problem.

4 THE VALIDITY OF MEASUREMENT

Problems of the validity of the measures used arise most frequently in those services such as social services and education where the outcomes of the service are multiple, not subject to widespread agreement, and not uniquely a consequence of the service provided. Thus in the case of school education there are clearly many different outcomes or end results with relatively little agreement existing as to their relative importance and priority. For example a range of social, economic and cultural factors influence an outcome measure such as the 'post-schooling destinations' of pupils making its use as a performance measure open to continuing debate.

Questions of validity also arise from different psychological attitudes towards the act of measurement itself which create a 'battleground' which is fought repeatedly in committee rooms and management teams. The combatants can be represented by those who take extreme positions in relation to the following propositions:

▽   what gets measured gets done
▽   measurement drives out the immeasurable.

Supporters of the first proposition tend to see performance measures as appropriate mechanisms for achieving hierarchical direction and control, to use them prescriptively as a basis for action, and to achieve conformance to organizational aims and objectives. They may also be more prepared to use measures which are incomplete or only broadly indicative of performance as a basis for decision making. Supporters of the second proposition are much more likely to be extremely cautious in their use of performance measures, to use them descriptively, as a basis for asking questions only, and to accept that each measure can be interpreted in many different ways. They may tend to pursue the development of more sophisticated measures at the expense of using the ones they have already got.

The two sets of 'supporters' are of course abstract characterizations. They do however represent quite different conflicting approaches to measurement which are often responsible for holding back its development.

5 A HISTORY OF PURPOSELESS DATA COLLECTION

The final psychological reaction to performance measurement which needs to be borne in mind when performance measures are being developed is that the attitude of many staff will be influenced by their experience of data collection in the past. For decades local authority staff have been required to collect, collate and report statistical data required by senior managers in their own departments, by central departments and by a multitude of government departments and agencies. That information is rarely used by those who collect it, nor in some cases, do they see it being used by others for any useful purpose. While it may be argued that local authority departments could have made more use of the information they collect for others, it appears that many have not. They have simply conformed with the requirement to collect it. As a consequence, initiatives in performance measurement may be met by an attitude of disbelief and indifference by those staff who are required to provide and collect the necessary data. To overcome this barrier it is necessary for those who are leading such initiatives to do three things:

▽   to demonstrate to those who have to undertake the sometimes tedious task of providing and compiling the data that it will be used
▽   to clarify and justify the use to which it will be put, and the context in which it will be used
▽   to create an organizational culture in which accountability is perceived as a necessary and appropriate condition of life, albeit a sometimes uncomfortable one, and where performance measurement is perceived as a proper mechanism for achieving accountability.

Developing a performance measurement system

Much of the literature on performance measurement is more informative about the methodology of measurement (that is, it helps to answer questions relating to *how* to measure and *what* to measure) than it is about either the purpose of measurement (i.e. the question of *why* measurement is being undertaken) or about the recipients and users of the measures (i.e. the questions of *who* they are for and what they are supposed to do with them). This approach is sometimes reflected in those local authorities which approach the development of performance measures by sifting through all their available data in order to determine what measures can be created in the often vague hope that they will be of some use. While the analysis and use of existing data sources is one important and pragmatic step in the development of a performance measurement system, it should not be the first step. First it is necessary to ascertain what the measures are to be used for, and by whom they are to be used.

What is the purpose of performance measurement?

There are a variety of purposes to which performance measures can be put, but not all performance measures can be used for a variety of purposes. The measure must relate to the purpose so that distortions in

judgement and decision are minimalized. Thus a measure of volume of
service provided is frequently of little relevance to the question of service
effectiveness, but in the absence of more appropriate information (e.g.
volume of service in relation to a prescribed or identified level of need) is
sometimes improperly used as an indicator of effectiveness.

David Mayston (1985) has identified nine potential roles for performance indicators in the public sector generally, all of which are relevant to
local authorities. They are:

▽ to help clarify the organization's objectives
▽ to evaluate the final outcomes resulting from the authority's activities
▽ as an input into managerial incentive schemes
▽ to enable consumers to make informed choices
▽ to indicate performance standards for contracted-out, licensed or privat-
  ized services
▽ to indicate the effectiveness with which different service activities in a
  given policy area contribute to a policy goal or objective
▽ as a trigger for further investigation and possible remedial action to
  improve the quality of inputs and outputs
▽ to assist in determining the most cost-effective set of service levels to
  attain a given target
▽ to indicate areas of potential cost saving.

Identifying a lack of effective use of available performance indicators as a
major problem to be overcome, Mayston proposes that one solution is 'a
clear identification of their potential role in the decision making process'.
If, within a local authority, decision-making roles are clear, being identified
within a well defined decision-making process such as that demonstrated
by the examples used in the previous chapter, then the problem is to a
large extent resolvable.

Who are the performance measures for?

Many approaches to performance measures have the appearance of
being essentially managerial in nature and are directed primarily at senior
managers and service committees. While this primary focus is both logical
and necessary, it can obscure the existence of many other potential users
whose interests need to be borne in mind. The following list is presented
as an indication of the variety of potential users rather than as a fully
comprehensive statement.

EXTERNAL USERS – NATIONAL

▽ Government Departments – to determine policies, allocate resources
▽ M.P.'s – for debate in parliament, etc
▽ Audit Commission – for audit analysis purposes
▽ Regulatory and Inspection Agencies – to fulfill their statutory roles
▽ National pressure, promotion and interest groups – e.g. national volun-
  tary agencies, CBI, Trade Unions

EXTERNAL USERS – LOCAL

▽   Voters and citizens generally – to inform themselves and make choices
▽   Users of services – to inform themselves, assess quality and value, and
    make choices
▽   Local M.P.s/M.E.P.s – to promote local interests and identify local
    problems
▽   Local pressure, promotion and interest groups – to inform themselves
    for a variety of purposes.

INTERNAL USERS – COUNCILLORS

▽   Local political party groups – to determine manifestos
▽   As corporate policy-makers and resource allocators
▽   As service committee members
▽   In a performance review role.

INTERNAL USERS – OFFICERS

▽   Corporate Management – Chief Executive and Chief Officers
▽   Corporate Resource Allocators and Controllers
▽   Corporate Policy Analysts and Reviewers
▽   Departmental Senior Management
▽   Cost and responsibility managers and budget holders
▽   Front line staff
▽   Trade Unions.

This lengthy list of possible users is not produced to suggest that each set
of users requires a unique set of performance measures to suit their needs.
That would clearly be impractical and unnecessary. But the list does serve
to illustrate that there are many groups with an interest or stake in local
government, that they each have some right to receive information about a
local authority's performance, and that the information they need, although
unlikely to be uniquely different for each group, will nonetheless differ
considerably in both content and format.

    The list also demonstrates the range of potential external users for
which a local authority is *required* to produce information. Information for
service users is increasingly being specified in detail by the Government,
and while the specification may be a necessary stimulus to those authorities
which have in the past been reluctant to provide any information, it may
form a constraint on those which are willing to provide their customers
with a fuller basis on which to make judgments about the value and quality
of services.

    The recent specification of performance indicators to be provided to
local authority housing tenants in accordance with the 1989 Local Government and Housing Act provides a good example of this problem. The
Consultation Paper issued by the Department of the Environment in October 1989, proposed a set of indicators heavily oriented towards measures
of volume, cost, economy and efficiency. Only one was concerned with
levels of tenant satisfaction and one further measure could be related to

the concept of effectiveness in an indirect way. Effectiveness was otherwise only dealt with in the limited sense that it was suggested that each indicator should have a target attached to it.

Two points of interest arise from this exercise: first, it is difficult to imagine how tenants would make use of some of the performance indicators, or whether they would wish to do so. The Consultation Paper contained no evidence to suggest that tenants had been consulted as to their need for information nor about what they considered to be the most important characteristic of housing management. A recent study on the quality of housing management carried out by Spencer and Walsh for the Joseph Rowntree Memorial Trust (1990) produced survey evidence that low rent levels were not regarded by tenants as the most important aspect of the housing service and that their priorities for service were primarily concerned with the qualities of the staff they dealt with and the nature of their interaction. Second, it was not surprising in these circumstances that the Association of Metropolitan Authorities expressed its suspicion about the Government's motives 'as the proposed performance indicators seem to be those that interest central government far more than they do local authority tenants' (AMA: Response to the DoE Consultation Paper: Published Performance Indicators for Local Authority Tenants).

Users and uses – constructing a basis for performance measurement

Analysing both the uses and users of performance measurement provides a basis for constructing an information system which produces relevant performance information for each group. By asking a series of questions it becomes possible to identify which performance measures should be reported to whom. The principal questions to be asked in relation to each group of internal users are:

▽ What activities/services are they responsible for?
▽ What decisions do they have to take and what information do they need to do so?
▽ What are the key characteristics of the service performance which they need to monitor?
▽ How frequently do decisions need to be taken and performance monitored?

For internal users the aim of this form of analysis should be to create a pyramid of performance measures which reflects the organizational and responsibility structure of the local authority. The principle is demonstrated by the Audit Commission's use of pyramids (see Figure 4.1) which in outline form relate users (by management level) to their purpose in using information and to the type and frequency of information required. As the Audit Commission points out, councillors can be considered as being at the top of the pyramid. They cannot and should not attempt to monitor all aspects of performance themselves and their role should therefore be to:

▽ 'monitor a limited set of measures that they judge to be most critical, supplemented with an annual review of the whole service'.

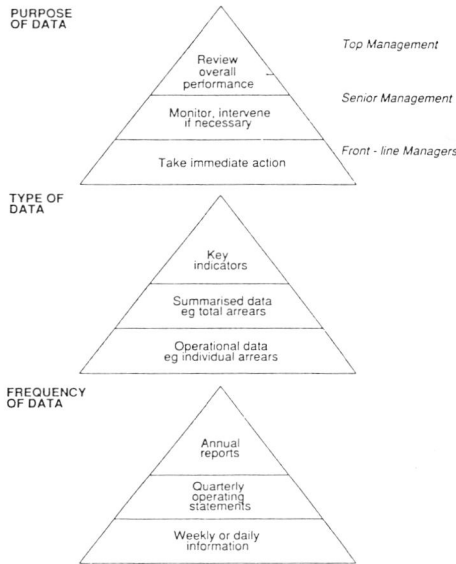

Figure 4.1 Responsibilities For monitoring – different managers need different information.
(Audit Commission 'Managing Services Effectively – Performance Review' 1989)

▽ 'ensure that officers are adequately monitoring everything else, at the appropriate detail and frequency'.
▽ 'require any deviations beyond a certain level of significance to be reported to them immediately'.
   (Audit Commission: Managing Services Effectively – Performance Review)

The same principles can be applied to each tier of management responsibility from chief officers to front-line managers and supervisors. Although a simplification of reality, the pyramid principle is a powerful conceptual tool which can be used as a basis for designing performance monitoring and reporting systems. Its value has been demonstrated by exercises such as that carried out by Wrekin District Council in the field of leisure services. Faced with a service for which it is possible to generate very large numbers of performance measures for each service facility, the department then reduced their indicators to a manageable and practical number and consulted with its managers as to their validity and usefulness.
   The performance indicators were stratified into three layers:

▽ Global Indicators (Frequency: annual) – such as the provision of particular facilities/activities per 1000 head of population. To be used for service planning.
▽ Service Review Indicators (Frequency: from weekly to annually depending on indicator) – to be used by on-site managers to help in decisions such as: determining staffing levels, highlighting areas needing promotion, indicating areas of excessive expenditure, etc.

```
INDICATOR              FORMULA/USE                    FREQUENCY
=========              ===========                    =========

PROVISION              - Open Space (hectares)        GLOBAL-Annual
                         ----------------------
                         1000 pop./Ward

                       - Area of open space per
                         person or ward constituent.

INCOME/COSTS           - *Income                      REVIEW-Quarterly
                         --------
                         *Costs   x 100%

                         Where *=From Recreational
                                  Facilities.

                       - Income as a % of
                         expenditure.

UTILISATION            - Usage Of Facilities          REVIEW-Quarterly
                         --------------------
                         Capacity          x 100%

                       - Usage of parks recreational
                         facilities as a % of
                         capacity.

QUALITY                - Compliments/complaints       REVIEW-Quarterly
                         dealing with:
                            Housing work
                            Floral displays
                            Horticultural features
                            Horticultural advice

% COMPARISONS          - This Years x                 MONITORING-Monthly
                         ------------
                         Last Years x

                         where x=Utilisation
                                =Income/Costs

                       - Comparisons with:
                            Targets
                            Previous years
                            Other parks
```

Figure 4.2 Stratifying performance indicators. An example from the Parks Service (Wrekin District Council)

▽ Operational Monitoring Indicators (Frequency: monthly or quarterly) – to provide comparisons of performance with targets, over-time and with other similar facilities.

An example of the resulting performance indicators for one service is given in Figure 4.2.

Performance measures can also be structured in relation to objectives where these are clearly stated. Thus the City of Westminster has structured its performance measurement system on the basis of its primary objective of 'building stable communities', which is achieved by means of five objectives which are applied to all services:

▽ improving the quality of life
▽ 'close to the customer'
▽ fulfilling statutory obligations
▽ maintaining a positive profile
▽ being run like a business (achieving its objectives efficiently and effectively).

Each objective is applied to each area of service and one or more performance measures used to monitor performance against each objective.

A basis for comparison

Simply to measure a particular characteristic of performance is often virtually meaningless unless it is compared to something else. To know that 10,000 books are borrowed from a branch library in a week may be of some interest but it is of little use in evaluating performance. To know that the cost of providing meals-on-wheels is £x per meal is information of a kind, but is not of great value to managers of the service unless they have some basis of comparison. Identifying a useful and meaningful basis for comparison is therefore essential in developing performance measures. For many services there are five different comparisions which can be made:

1 TIME

A comparison with last week, month or year is the most easily available and commonly used comparitor which can be used to analyse most characteristics of performance. Time comparisons become particularly useful for analysing trends over a period of months or years. Some measures such as consumer satisfaction/dissatisfaction rates become much more meaningful once trends are identified.

2 TARGETS

A performance-oriented local authority is likely to have set targets for all activities which make a significant contribution to a major objective. Targets may be expressed in a variety of ways, including:

▽   cost and economy targets (e.g. % cost reduction targets)
▽   efficiency and productivity targets (e.g. % occupancy rates for residential houses)
▽   output or volume targets (e.g. number of users of a sports facility).
▽   activity completion dates.

Targets of effectiveness, outcome and quality have been less frequently used, but may include measures such as:

▽   % reduction in customer complaints resulting from faulty work.
▽   % of trainees entering appropriate employment within six months of completion of training.

3 INTRA-SERVICE

An extremely valuable form of comparison where a service is provided through a number of separate organizational units, such as schools, residential homes, housing area/estate offices. While issues of the validity of comparisons will arise they will not be as difficult to overcome as in the case of inter-authority comparisons. Intra-service comparisons are also more useful in analysing the extent of achievement of policy objectives and can more readily be analysed and interpreted in order to understand the causes of different levels of performance.

4 INTER-AUTHORITY

There now exists a considerable amount of information by way of national averages, yardsticks, standards and benchmarks produced by

CIPFA, the Audit Commission, Government Departments, HMIs and by other national bodies. More discrete comparisons can also be made using the Audit Commission's 'families' or where a local authority selects its own 'family' of authorities – Oxfordshire County Council has, for example, carried out a comparative study with neighbouring county councils over a number of years. Problems of the validity of comparison inevitably arise, particularly with regard to effectiveness, and available comparisons tend to be limited to cost, volume, economy and efficiency.

5 OTHER ORGANIZATIONS AND INSTITUTIONS

For certain activities and services comparators may exist elsewhere in the public, private and voluntary sectors. Professional and commercial fee rates are amongst the most commonly used comparisons of this kind but others, such as residential and social work costs in the voluntary sector, also exist. Support services, such as transport costs, may also be compared in this way. Compulsory competition and service level agreements have made this type of comparison more relevant and more acceptable in many local authorities.

Presentation of performance measures

The level of numeracy skills found amongst local authority managers and councillors, and amongst the public generally, is extremely variable. The straight presentation of numbers in tabular form renders them almost incomprehensible to some users. The use, therefore, of different forms of visual presentation such as graphs, histograms, scattergrams and pie charts, can make them much more meaningful and useful. Figure 4.3 contains some simple examples.

New information technology, especially the availability of relatively cheap and easy-to-use graphics software programmes, makes the improved presentation of numerical information a much simpler, more flexible and efficient process than in the past.

The value of such developments is well illustrated by the development of performance indicator reports in the Social Services Department of Westminster City Council. In the first stage of development managers were provided with performance indicators presented in rows and columns of numbers. The information was important but its presentation not particularly user-friendly. The second stage of development resulted in the information being presented much more clearly in graph and chart formats, but with the previous presentation format still being available on request by those managers who preferred or needed it.

What to measure? – analytical frameworks for distinguishing different characteristics of performance

It was suggested earlier that the three E's constituted a 'new orthodoxy' of performance measurement. That statement must now be severely qualified, for while there does exist a general agreement as to the analytical framework which should be used for performance measurement, there

Budget Monitoring

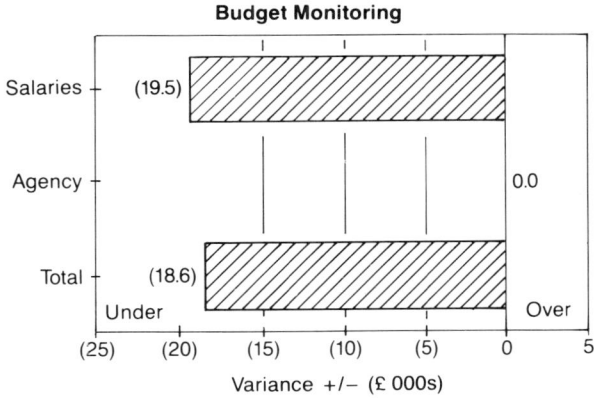

**Priority Homeless Cases 1987/88
by Family Composition**

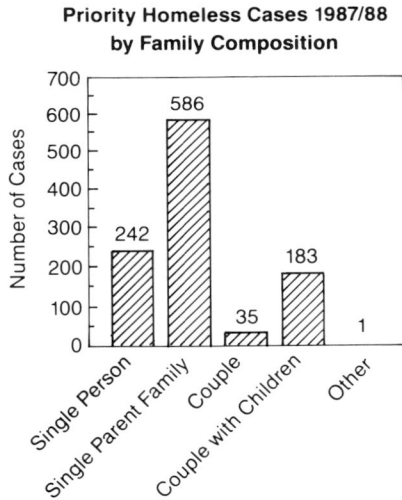

Development Dept Work Programme 89/90

"Live" Tasks Performance (Sept 89)

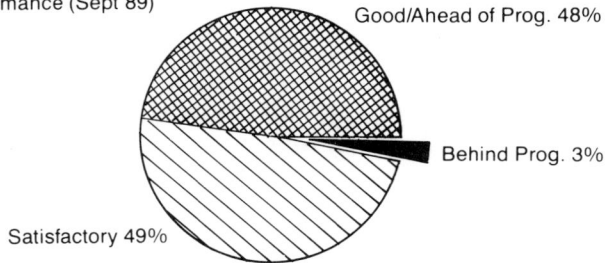

Figure 4.3 Making data more user friendly – some simple examples

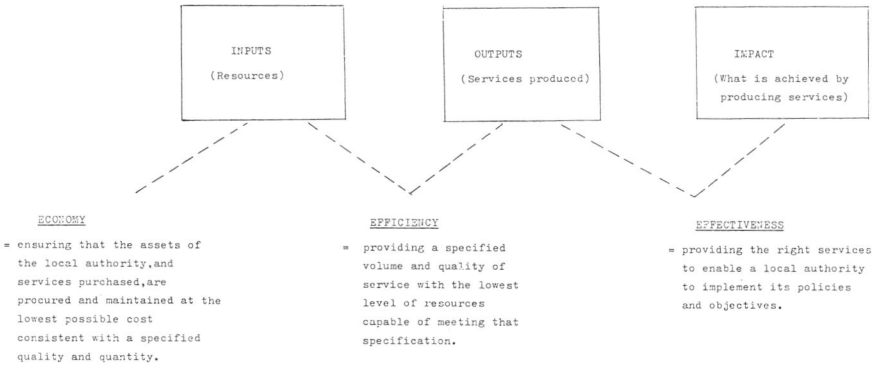

```
┌──────────────────┐        ┌──────────────────┐        ┌──────────────────┐
│      INPUTS      │        │     OUTPUTS      │        │      IMPACT      │
│                  │        │                  │        │                  │
│   (Resources)    │        │(Services produced)│       │ (What is achieved by │
│                  │        │                  │        │ producing services)  │
└──────────────────┘        └──────────────────┘        └──────────────────┘
```

ECONOMY

= ensuring that the assets of
the local authority,and
services purchased,are
procured and maintained at the
lowest possible cost
consistent with a specified
quality and quantity.

EFFICIENCY

= providing a specified
volume and quality of
service with the lowest
level of resources
capable of meeting that
specification.

EFFECTIVENESS

= providing the right services
to enable a local authority
to implement its policies
and objectives.

Figure 4.4 The three E's (definitions used are those provided by the Audit Commission in 1986)

remain a number of conceptual differences as well as numerous problems in the practical application of the concepts.

Economy, efficiency and effectiveness

The three E's remain the best starting point for analysing performance because they are based on an apparently clear model of what can be measured, as illustrated in Figure 4.4.

The problem with this apparently clear model stems from the concept of 'effectiveness'. By defining it as 'providing the right services to enable the local authority to implement its policies and objectives', the Audit Commission avoids two problems. First, there is the question of whether that definition really addresses the concepts of the impact, the effect, or (to use another admittedly ambiguous word) the consequences, of local authority activity; secondly, it begs the question of how local authorities state their objectives. If they are stated in terms of intended impact, effect or consequence then the definition is acceptable. But frequently that is not the case and objectives can be expressed simply in terms of the volume of service to be provided. The objectives of some services may be expressed in terms of what the Audit Commission defines as 'efficiency' – i.e. providing a specified volume and quality of service with the lowest level of resources capable of meeting that requirement – and as a consequence the concept of effectiveness becomes simply the achievement of efficiency. The definition may have been a reflection of the Government's primary goal of achieving greater economy and efficiency or it may have resulted from the

MEASURING PERFORMANCE

Performance is measured at four main levels

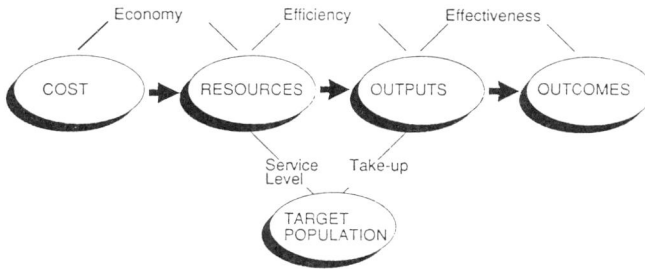

Figure 4.5 A Development of the three E's model of performance.
(Audit Commission 'Managing Services Effectively – Performance Review'
1989)

Audit Commission's awareness of the problems involved in establishing clear causal relationships between outputs and effects.

By 1989 the Audit Commission had redefined its basic model and its definitions of the three E's in a way which reflected a growing concern with effectiveness and quality. The model now contained four dimensions of measurement (see Figure 4.5), two of which, cost and resources, are self evident. Outputs were defined as:

▽ 'the use made of resources or the service actually delivered to the public'.

Outcomes were defined as:

▽ 'the ultimate value or benefit of the service to its users' and as 'meeting users' needs or achieving its underlying purpose'.

The three E's were now defined in the following terms:

▽ Economy measures – 'the cost of acquiring resources such as staff premises or supplies' (essentially no change from the earlier definition)
▽ Efficiency measures – 'the outputs achieved in relation to the resource inputs'. This definition was intended to include measures such as occupancy and utilization rates, and, presumably, productivity rates (the main distinction between this and the previous definition is that efficiency is now stated in descriptive rather than objective terms).
▽ Effectiveness – 'measures . . . of the final outcome of a service in relation to its output' (a broader definition than used previously).

In addition, the Commission highlighted the importance of identifying target (or catchment) populations for each service in order to produce two further measures:

▽ level of service – i.e. volume of service in relation to the target catchment population.
▽ take-up – i.e. proportion of target catchment population using the service – a measure which is suggested as a useful proxy indicator of the quality of service provided.

While it is possible to criticize the model, it is a useful attempt to provide an improved conceptual basis for developing performance measurement.

Other definitions of the dimensions of performance measurement

The literature of performance measurement is filled with conflicting and hence confusing concepts. Inputs, process, activity, intermediate outputs, throughput, onput, outcome, impact and consequences are all used by different authors as concepts defining the basis of measurement. There is no precise agreement even though many of the concepts used are very similar. Some of the differences may be no more than terminological in nature, and one is forced to ask whether it really matters. The most important thing is for a local authority to use a model and a set of definitions which are meaningful and on which it can reach agreement. Achieving conceptual and terminological agreement across local authorities, although of importance for making inter-authority comparisons, is of secondary importance.

The development of local models sometimes requires the abandonment of the language of the three E's, or its translation into a language and set of concepts which is more meaningful in particular local contexts. The London Borough of Richmond, for example, in providing advice to its managers on the development of performance indicators for use in annual management reports, suggests that the starting point should be to ask: what is important about each service provided – from the point of view of managers, members and customers? While acknowledging that the precise answers to that question, and therefore the performance indicators which result from it, will vary considerably from service to service, managers are advised that there are four key subsidiary questions which have to be addressed:

▽ Is the service cost-effective? – which is defined specifically, although unusually, in terms of particular aspects of economy and efficiency – i.e. unit costs, staffing levels and productivity ratios.
▽ Is the service provided/job done on time? – This question is highlighted as being a key indicator of quality used by customers of services.
▽ Is the service provided/job done 'properly'? – The definition of 'properly' is left for managers to determine.
▽ Is the customer satisfied? Stress is also placed on this question because of its high political profile, and managers are prompted to use the results of the authority's MORI surveys, to analyse complaints and to conduct their own customer survey or feedback exercises where appropriate.
(London Borough of Richmond – 1988 Annual Management Report Programme: Author's Notes)

The overall impression of this approach is that it very much reflects the main political objectives and interests of the authority. It also reflects the general approach to corporate management by providing a framework within which managers of individual services have some degree of flexibility.

Cambridgeshire County Council, in developing a corporate approach

```
                         THE MODEL - SERVICE X

           NEEDS
                    - the problems which give rise to the
                      Council's objectives and actions
                    - can also be seen as "opportunities"
                    - factors which shape the "market" in
                      in which we operate

           INPUTS
                    - resources consumed in the activity      --
                    - expressed in money terms as the          |
                      "common denominator"                     |
                    - expenditure per capita and/or unit       |
                      costs with comparisons where available   |
                                                    > EFFICIENCY --
                                                    |  RATIOS       |
           OUTPUTS                                  |               |
                    - the volume of "service delivered"        |    COST-
                                                    |         | EFFECTIVENESS
                    - the quality of that service,    --      >    or
                      eg staff qualifications, response time -- | VALUE FOR
                                                    |           | MONEY
                                                    |               |
                                                    |               |
           OUTCOMES                                 > EFFECTIVE- --
                                                    | NESS RATIOS
                    - how the needs change          |
                    - the impact of our activities  |
                    - including the client's opinion |
                                                    --



                         PRINCIPLES

           1   FOCUS ON EFFECTIVENESS

           2   CUSTOMER ORIENTATION

           3   COMPARISONS OVER TIME

           4   ONLY INDICATORS

           5   'GAPS' ACCEPTABLE
```

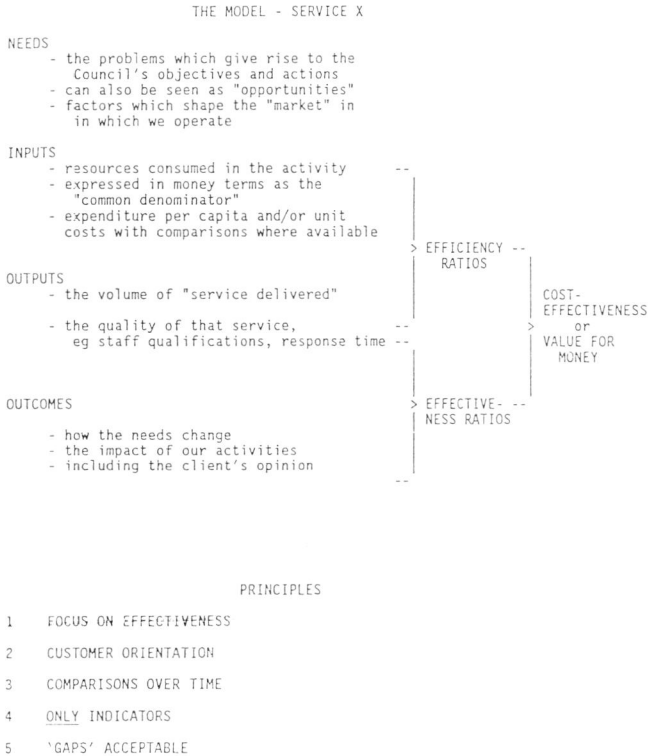

Figure 4.6 An example of a model used to develop performance indicators (Cambridgeshire County Council Performance Indicators Group 1988)

to performance indicators, have developed an approach which is close to the input-output-outcome model, but which reflects the importance of specifying the needs at which services are directed (see Figure 4.6). Miller's model for social services (see Figure 4.7) provides a more analytical basis for developing performance indicators, but requires a more sophisticated level of data collection than is available in most local authorities.

No one model is right for all purposes. The most important consideration is to provide a basis for measurement which is sufficiently simple to be readily understood while at the same time acknowledging the key factors which contribute to the performance of a service.

Consumers and citizens

The models of performance used so far in this chapter are dominated, not just by the language of accountants and economists, but by a process of thinking which defines the role of the local authority as a producer of

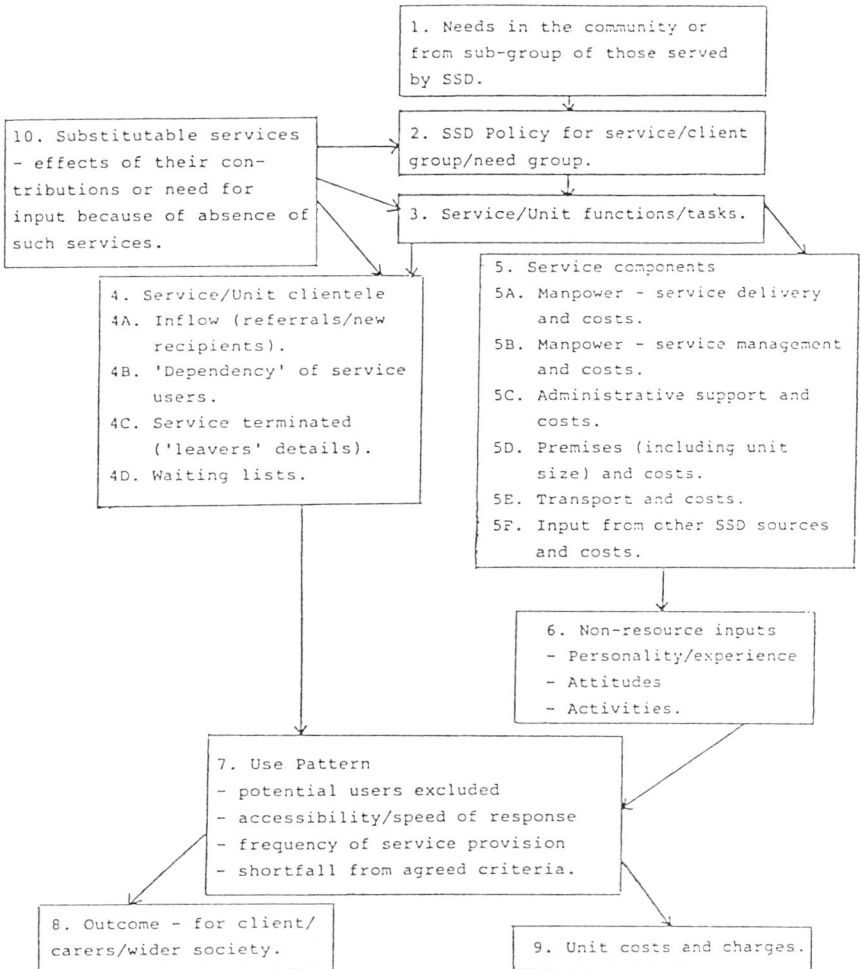

Figure 4.7 An example of a more complex model for deriving performance measures for Social Services.
(**N. Miller: 'Management Information and Performance Measurement in the Personal Social Services'** in *Social Services Research*: **1986 Nos 4 & 5 Dept of Social Admin, University of Birmingham**)

goods and services. It therefore naturally focuses on the process of converting resources into goods and services. Within this model organizational
performance is defined primarily in terms of services produced, rather than
in terms of services received by the customer or consumer. The lack of
measures of effectiveness, outcome or impact is not therefore surprising
and cannot simply be ascribed to the technical and conceptual problems
of measurement, even though these are undoubtedly important. If the
measurement of service, quality and effectiveness is to achieve any significant role in the overall measurement of performance then a model of
performance is required which provides an explicit focus on the interaction
between producers and receivers of services. The creation of such a model
must be considered as more than a purely technical process of analysis and
refinement of existing models. It is dependent on a more fundamental
change in the attitudes and cultures of local authorities with regard to the
respective roles and relationships between the local authority and its customers and citizens.

   That change is already taking place in a significant way. 'Customer
care', 'a public service orientation', 'close to the customer' and 'putting
people first', are all terms now widely used in local government. They have
been central to a whole range of new initiatives by local authorities, which
includes programmes of devolved management, the physical decentralization of services, customer care training for staff, improving physical access
to council buildings, public opinion polls, user surveys and the use of
marketing techniques. The use of the word 'customer' itself implies (or at
least is intended to imply) a new relationship – a 'customer' has rights and
the power of choice whereas a 'client' rarely has either, being subservient
to the professional provider of services.

   The concept of customers and their importance in both defining and
assessing the performance of local authority services is therefore gaining
ground and its impact on the measurement of performance occurs in several
ways.

Discovering the views of consumers and citizens

   The importance of obtaining information about what the public need
and want from a local authority and what they think about its services and
policies is now quite widely recognized in local government. Market
research techniques such as public opinion polls and user surveys are used
by large numbers of local authorities, the majority of which are directed
at assessing the level of public satisfaction or dissatisfaction with council
services. While the use of such surveys is enormously encouraging in
terms of indicating much greater potential responsiveness to consumers and
citizens, a number of questions arise as to their purpose, design and real
use.

The purpose of surveys

   As the LGTB's publication 'Getting Closer to the Public' points out,
before attempting to consult the public a local authority must be clear
about three things:

∇   what it is trying to find out
∇   whose views it wishes to seek
∇   the use it wishes to make of the information

With respect to each question the authority has a wide set of choices open to it. Being clear as to purpose will help determine whose views need to be obtained and how this can best be done. The way in which the information might be used will depend on why the information was required in the first place. The interconnections between these issues and questions is represented in outline in Figure 4.8.

Within the context of this variety of aims and methods, public opinion polls which identify general satisfaction levels, although they have attracted considerable attention and visibility, can be considered as only a limited step towards consumer measurement and assessment of services – a form of lowest common denominator. Their actual and potential limitations arise from a number of causes which require exploration.

In the first instance it is not always clear why local authorities use them. If the most limited and questionable purpose of customer service campaigns is to produce a 'service with a smile' syndrome or the charm school of service, then the most limited use of public opinion polls is as a public relations exercise. Unless public opinion polls are used in a demonstrable way to influence decisions and the way in which decisions are taken it may be assumed that they are simply public relations devices or that they are undertaken only because it is considered to be fashionable to do so. It may be argued that they can have a symbolic value within the local authority and that their influence is pervasive and generalized, and therefore not easy to demonstrate, but there is a danger (of which there is some evidence) that public opinion poll results can quickly achieve bottom-drawer status, being rapidly tucked away out of sight and mind.

Secondly, there is the problem which results from their often generalized nature. Overall averages of satisfaction and dissatisfaction fail to distinguish between the views and needs of different groups within the population. Such groups, whether they be geographic, social or ethnic, frequently receive different levels of service from the local authority, may have particular views and needs, and in some cases may be under-represented in the decision-making processes of the local authority. Global averaging of satisfaction levels and other measures tells the local authority little about its relationship with particular groups and does little to raise the question of equity of provision, a concept which may be considered to be equally important as the three E's previously referred to. The question of who benefits from a local authority's service is of vital importance to the general concept of performance.

A further problem arises from the practice of those local authorities who carry out only one isolated public opinion poll at one point in time. In such cases, it is often difficult to read, interpret and attach significance to particular results. The fact that 95% of the population are satisfied with library lending services may justifiably cause a sense of satisfaction in a library committee and department, but it is only of limited use. Knowing that satisfaction levels have increased or decreased over a period of time is much more useful and therefore the repeated use of surveys is of import-

You want to find out what your public thinks of the service with which you are most concerned.

Why do you want this information? For example, is it to:
- help you allocate resources, fix budgets, make sensitive cuts etc
- determine policies and priorities for the service
- assess needs, preference and expectations
- redesign the service
- market the service
- explore the service's image
- evaluate performance as perceived by customers or citizens
- establish that you care about people's views
- some other reason?

Whose views would you seek:
- users
- people who might use the service, but don't
- 'unwilling customers'
- any priority groups your authority has identified
- people indirectly affected by the service
- taxpayers and ratepayers
- electors
- everyone who lives/works/studies in the area ('the general public')
- visitors
- professionals involved in providing the service
- staff in contact with the public
- all staff
- the voluntary sector
- the business community
- others?

What would you ask them about? (You may want to ask different things of different people.) These are some of the aspects of service you might wish to cover:
- awareness of services
- actual use made
- reasons for not using services
- relevance to need/appropriateness to individuals and groups
- perceived equity between consumers
- access/accessibility (geographical and physical)
- image
- quality factors, for example speed, reliability, range of facilities/services, staff expertise etc
- ease and pleasantness of use, including public/ staff contact and environmental factors
- convenience
- provision of information to aid choice/awareness/use
- complaints and complaints-handling
- representation and participation; extent to which the public can:
  - make choices
  - communicate views
  - participate in decisions
- cost to user and to community
- effectiveness: benefits/outcomes for individual and community.

What else would you ask people?

What method(s) would you choose to find out the views of the different 'publics' you have identified? The table on p27 may help you decide.
- using complaints, commendations and suggestions
- studying demand
  - looking at use
  - test marketing
- talking to representative groups
- conducting market research
  - quantitative
  - qualitative
- introducing user democracy:
  - extending customer choice
  - user control
  - holding a referendum
- changing structures
- listening to front-line staff.

How would you *use* the information you have collected?

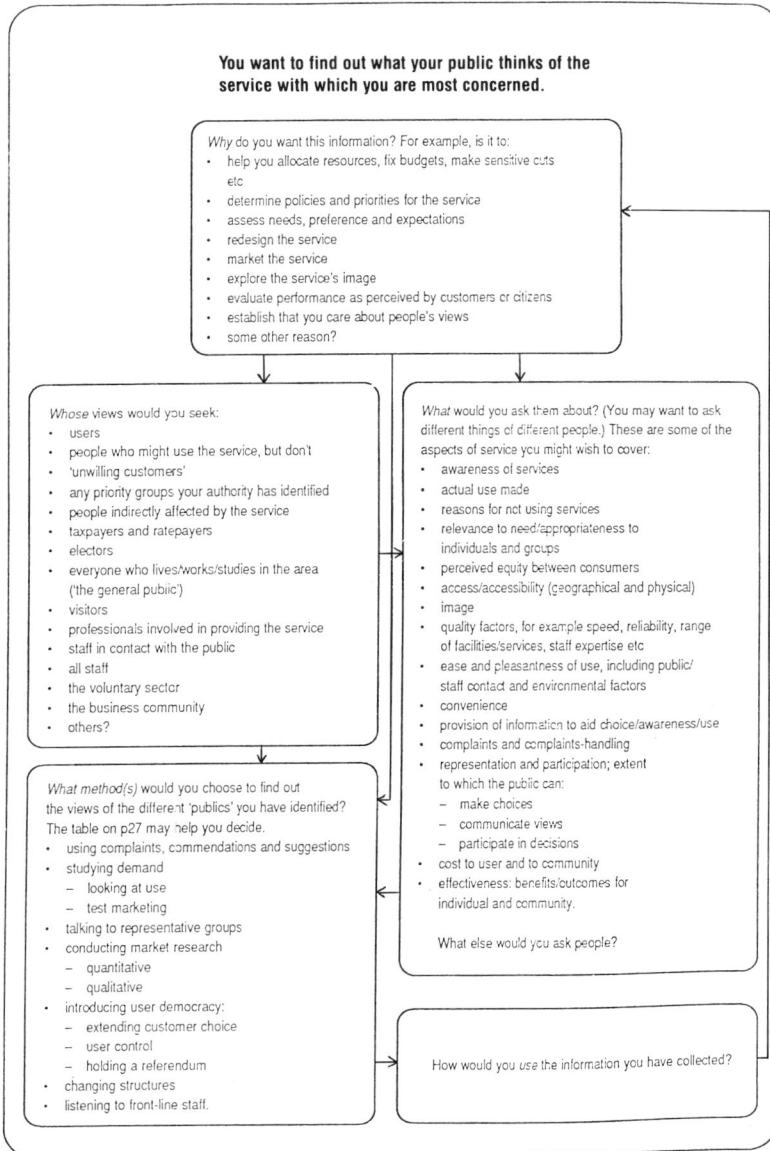

Figure 4.8 Consulting the public – questions for clarifying purpose, method, content and use.
(Local Government Training Board Getting Closer to The Public 1987)

ance in enabling the local authority to build up trends in consumer views. The provision of comparative information in reports by large polling organizations such as MORI goes some way towards overcoming the limitations of one-off surveys, but they generally remain difficult to interpret with confidence, and therefore can be easily dismissed.

Finally, there is the problem of how one-off surveys are fed into the decision-making machinery. Because they are not part of the normal systems, procedures and culture of a local authority, there may be no clear process for ensuring they are appropriately considered and used. They may be circulated within the authority without ever playing a role in the key arenas of decision-making. In at least one authority the author has found evidence that even senior managers have not examined the results of a survey published over a year previously.

Limitations such as these are not common to all local authorities, many of which have refined, developed and integrated their use of public opinion polls in a variety of ways, as the following examples help illustrate:

▽ Cleveland County Council has developed the most systematic and continuous approach to surveying the public's views. Starting in 1975, the authority has regularly conducted citizen's surveys. Using a random sample of 2,200 residents, they have built up a quite unique record of public opinion which allows them to analyse trends in opinion in relation to their own decisions about policy, resource allocation and service provision. Because the survey is an integrated part of the decision-making process, the authority has the capacity to use the results of the survey to make changes in policies and in resource allocation to particular services. While the initial focus of the social monitoring process was on general satisfaction levels, as it has developed and its value become recognized, it has increasingly moved towards addressing specific service questions which are requested by departments within the Council, and by District Councils. The ethos of obtaining the public's views has been further extended by focusing on particular groups within the community, as is demonstrated by the use of a survey of unemployed people as part of the development of an unemployment strategy.

▽ the London Borough of Richmond-upon-Thames has also developed a strategic and integrated approach to the use of public and customer surveys. The impact of surveys conducted by MORI in 1984 and 1986 was not just to provide the Council with better information on which to base its decisions. It established the principle of collecting trend data from regular surveys, and the political importance attached to the results caused some departments to undertake their own surveys and to be generally more active in obtaining feedback from customers. Since then the Council has developed a strategy for obtaining the public's views which involves regular sample surveys of residents, service user surveys and surveys of key customer groups.

▽ Humberside County Council has also adopted a comprehensive approach which supports a Public Service Orientation initiative. In addition to a household survey, interviews and surveys have also been undertaken in two libraries, two social services neighbourhood team areas and in parts of the Education and Technical Services Departments. Apart from obtaining information about general levels of satisfaction and use, the surveys have also focused on questions of awareness, access and treatment of service users.

Many of the above examples consist of specially conducted surveys which require special resources and expertise. A number of local authorities have established the practice of more closely relating the gathering of consumer views to the process of service delivery itself. These include the use of simple self-completion questionnaires at the point of service delivery for services such as libraries, leisure centres and housing offices, and reply-cards used to signify the completion of a service and to comment upon it.

Public measurement of performance

The preceding section may be described as being concerned with performance measurement *by* the public. The increasing use of surveys and questionnaires has gone some way towards extending local government's concept and understanding of its own performance, but the full effect of this change will not be felt unless the criteria which customers and citizens use to judge and measure performance are integrated with those used by the local authority itself – a process which may be described as performance measurement *for* the public.

Trying to achieve this integration is not easy, for, as acknowledged by the National Consumer Council, practice is not as clear as theory. 'Measuring Up', the N.C.C.'s report of their analysis of six services in Cambridgeshire and Newcastle upon Tyne, does however contain numerous valuable ideas and practical suggestions for bringing customers and their views into the local authority performance measurement process, of which four require exploration.

1 IDENTIFYING CONSUMER CRITERIA

The importance of identifying and responding to the criteria which consumers use to evaluate the services they receive is central to the development of performance measurement. The N.C.C.'s development of the Service Wheel (see Figure 4.9) has provided a powerful analytical framework for helping local authorities commence this process. The five core questions at the centre of the wheel can be applied to all services. They may however need to be supplemented by additional questions depending on the type of service being analysed, as will the definition and type of criteria used. Perhaps the most important contribution of the Service Wheel is to stress the importance of asking questions as part of the process of identifying performance measures, and in particular to start by asking questions which identify which aspects of a service are most important to them.

Consumer criteria for service evaluation

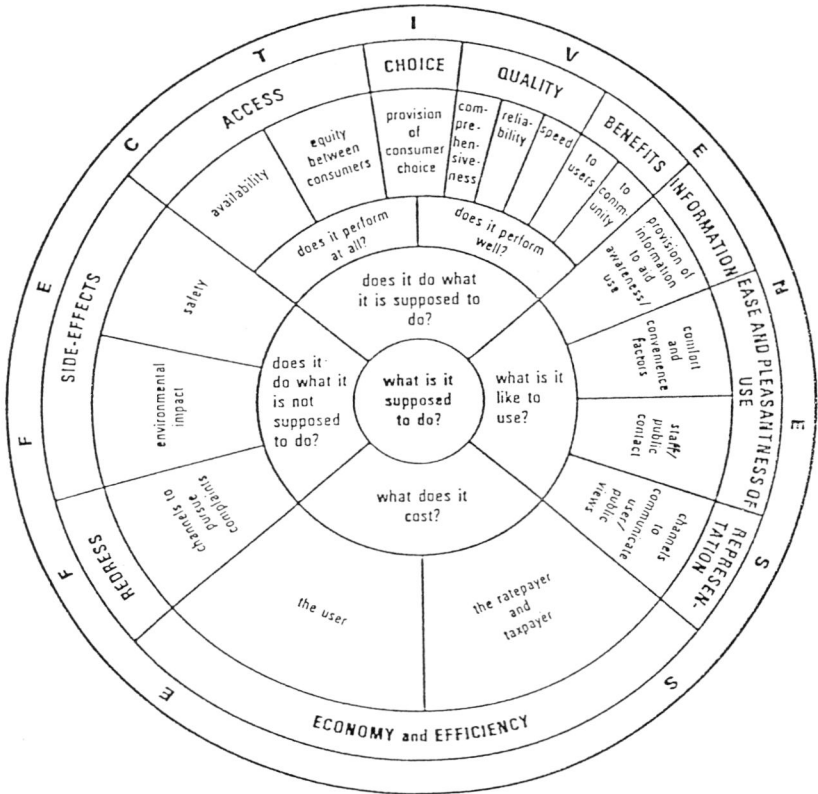

Figure 4.9 The 'Service Wheel'
(The National Consumer Council 'Measuring Up' 1986)

2 QUALITATIVE AS WELL AS QUANTITATIVE MEASUREMENT

The N.C.C. stress the need for local authorities to use a variety of qualitative and quantitative methods to evaluate services and make the important point that:

> A qualitative evaluation set within a broad statistical context seems the most promising way of investigating a service's achievement and those people who favour either 'hard' statistics or 'softer' evaluative data appear to assume that the two are mutually exclusive when their strength lies in their combination. (N.C.C. 'Measuring Up' 1986)

In practice many of the arguments about the use of soft or hard data emerge more from a resistance to accept external evaluation of performance than from any real analysis of the validity of the measures themselves. 'Hard' and 'objective' can be used as euphemisms for data which the local authority or department generate internally, and therefore has control over, while 'soft' and 'subjective' are euphemisms for data generated externally.

3 NEGATIVE PERFORMANCE INDICATORS

The N.C.C. states as one of its ten principles of performance measurement that:

> The number and nature of complaints can be used to assess satisfaction with services, even if imperfectly. Local authorities should take a more positive view of complaints. This involves actively seeking them out, analysing their causes, and feeding information back into the process of performance planning and review. (N.C.C. 'Measuring Up' 1986)

This principle raises two important points, the first being the importance of consumer redress as an important characteristic of public service and as a criterion by which consumers evaluate performance. The importance of providing and publicising a method of redress is now increasingly recognized, and local authorities have responded by producing two general types of information:

▽   Information leaflets on individual services, which not only describe the service and how and where to obtain it, but also inform the public of their rights to the service, the standard of service they can expect and the means by which they can complain. Customer and Service Contracts are an extension of this process and are discussed below.
▽   Complaints leaflets which inform the public of matters such as: how they can complain; who they should complain to; the procedures for dealing with complaints and the length of time they may take; other avenues of complaint such as the Ombudsman and councillors.

Complaints are only one example of what are often referred to as Negative Indicators, that is, indicators of what should not happen. In a supermarket, empty shelves may be used as an indicator of poor performance. Post-operative mortality is a negative indicator for hospitals. As a way of focusing attention on what may be a significantly poor aspect of performance, negative performance indicators can fill an important role. To be alerted to the fact that 5% of pot-holes are not repaired within one year of being reported may be more important than to know that 50% are repaired within one month. Complaints, although an indirect measure, can through their careful monitoring and analysis, alert local authorities to important performance failures.

Negative indicators conform to the principle of exception reporting – i.e. that managers should only receive information about those exceptions where performance has strayed outside previously defined parameters, and where corrective action needs to be taken. They are a useful way of reducing the volume of data which needs to be reported.

4 QUALITY OF SERVICE

The concept of quality is in many ways central to the concept of consumer evaluation of services advanced by the N.C.C. It is a concept which is more likely to be used by consumers than notions of economy, efficiency and effectiveness. It is also a concept which, at the general level at least, might be expected to be embraced by local authority staff, many of whom feel, justifiably or not, that economy and efficiency has been pursued at the expense of quality of service they are able to provide. The ethos and idea of public service, on which many staff in local government lay personal stress, is expressed more frequently in terms which are related to quality than to efficiency and effectiveness. Whether that concept of quality has in the past been sufficiently defined or demonstrated in ways which are recognized and accepted by consumers is open to considerable doubt. That however is not the point. What is of relevance now is the fact that the conditions of local government have sufficiently changed to bring about a shift in attitude and culture which creates the opportunity of using the concept of quality as a means of bringing together political, professional, technical, administrative and consumer and citizen criteria of performance in a way which has not been previously possible.

To be useful, quality needs to be given precise meaning in relation to each service in order for it to be useful as a concept for developing performance measures, or indeed for more broadly determining what services should be provided and in what way. The N.C.C. Service Wheel identifies comprehensiveness, reliability and speed as characteristics of quality. That suggests a narrower concept of quality than many might wish to use, and there may be many more relevant characteristics.

The tasks of specifying and measuring quality are already being addressed in a variety of ways in local authorities. Compulsory competitive tendering and service level agreements have created the need to specify quality of service. While local authorities have often found difficulty in achieving this, examples such as the inclusion in contracts of customer complaints monitoring and technical specifications of quality such as the nutritional value of meals are not uncommon. The use of service level agreements within local authorities has also prompted many central departments to find out from service departments what services they require and what their criteria of quality are.

Accuracy, availability and speed of delivery are frequently found to be important characteristics. In other services, the concept of quality is achieving greater relevance. In social services departments for example, much greater precision has been achieved in defining and specifying the meaning of Quality of Life, Quality of Care and Quality of Management in residential homes for elderly people. In a recent publication from the Social Services Inspectorate (1989), prepared by a team including staff from six local authorities, the means for evaluating and measuring the quality of life experienced and the quality of care provided are expressed in great detail within a matrix: one axis of this comprises statements of the key values which contribute to the quality of life (Privacy; Dignity; Independence; Choice; Rights; Fulfillment) while the second axis comprises the main features of the service provided (Physical Environment; Care Practices; Staff; Staff Training and Development; Procedures; Case Records; Documents; Meals and Meal Times).

At a more general level, the analysis of quality in local government services has been assisted by authors such as Stewart and Walsh. They draw an important distinction between the delivery of services and the production of manufactured goods:

> Quality in manufactured goods is easier to define than in a service because the experience of using the physical goods is separate from the process of production.
> (Stewart, J. and Walsh, K. (1989). The Search for Quality).

For many, but not all, local authority services, the processes of production and consumption are closely linked, with the user being part of the production process. In Education, Social Services and many enforcement services 'the user is a necessary and inextricable part of the process of service production'.

Having established the importance of the producer-consumer relationship, Stewart and Walsh then provide a framework for analysing quality which can be used for analysing and specifying quality and for identifying quality measures for individual services. The framework operates at three levels:

▽ the core service as fitness for purpose – that is 'whether the service does what it is designed to do' and 'meets the requirements for those for whom it is provided'
▽ the service surroundings – that is whether the physical conditions within which the service is provided 'support and enhance the service experience'
▽ the service relationship – that is the extent to which the personal relationship between the provider and receiver supports and enhances the service experience

The value of this form of analysis is that it requires service providers to consider the requirements of users as well as their own technical and professional specifications. Although it cannot be assumed that this approach will lead to the development of precise, quantified measures and standards, it helps point service providers in the direction of a more extended analysis of quality.

A more direct challenge to the need to produce consumer-oriented targets and performance measures has been the development of Customer Contracts. Stimulated by the Labour Party's publication of 'Quality Street', several authorities have piloted customer contracts for certain services. The London Borough of Islington's contract includes the following information:

▽ the frequency of rubbish collection
▽ the day when rubbish will be collected
▽ the hours between which refuse will be collected
▽ where the refuse bin will be collected from and returned to
▽ arrangements for collection in bank holiday weeks
▽ who to contact if the council fails to empty a refuse bin on the appointed day
▽ a guarantee to empty a missed bin within 48 hours of notification
▽ who to contact if a new bin is needed or if an elderly or disabled resident has difficulty moving a bin to the appropriate collection point
▽ who to contact to make a formal complaint.
(The Labour Party: A Good Deal 1990)

York City Council has piloted a customer contract for street cleaning which includes a statement about frequency of service and a procedure for complaints which includes a promise to inform the complainant how their complaint was being dealt with. The London Borough of Newham has developed an Area Public Service Statement for five environmental services, which covers public highways, refuse collection, housing maintenance, maintenance of landscaped areas and snow clearance. The statement contains detailed specifications of minimum standards. The statement also invites people to complain and a promise is given to revise the statement from time to time. In addition, it includes a section in ethnic minority languages.

While these examples of customer contracts include certain information which cannot be considered new or novel, in various ways they successfully achieve more precise definitions of quality and more explicit procedures for redress than have existed previously.

A revised model of performance?

While all diagrammatic representations of complex situations tend towards over-simplification, they also have a value in highlighting key issues. The diagram contained in Figure 4.10 is not put forward as a schematic representation of all the issues concerning the measurement of performance which have been raised in this chapter. It is, however, intended as an improvement on the production-based model used earlier to demonstrate the relationship between the three E's. Amongst other things, it aims to include:

▽ the importance of identifying needs and expectations within the local community
▽ the recognition that performance measurement is set within a political context
▽ the concept of quality of service as defined at the point of service delivery by both producer and consumer

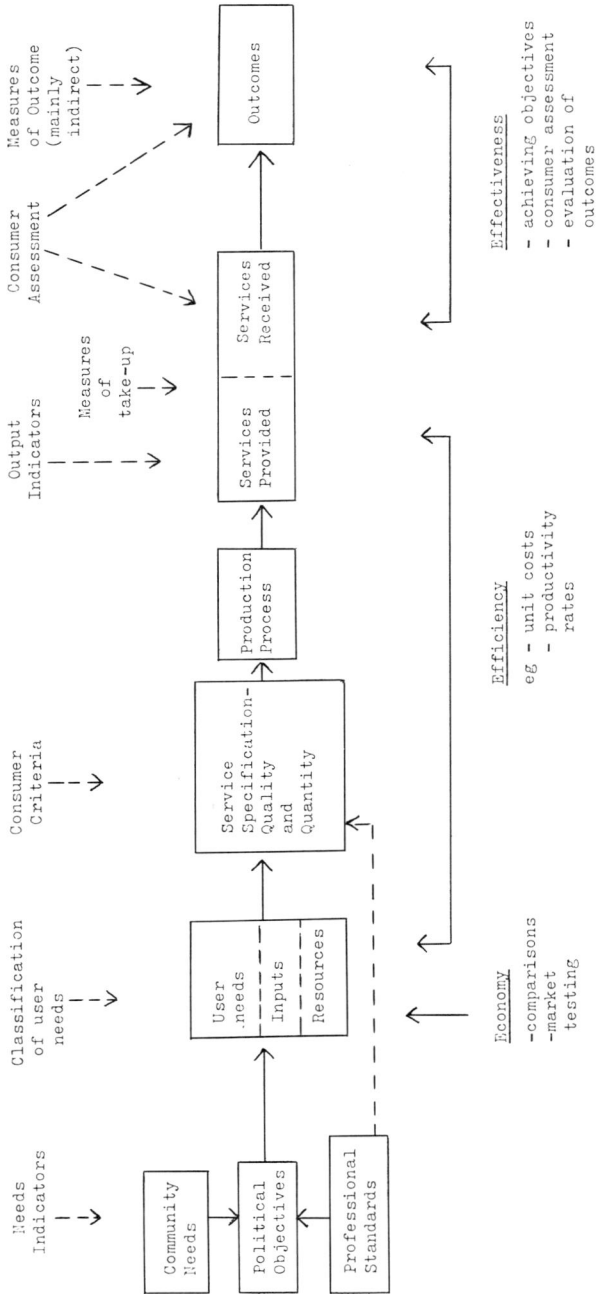

Figure 4.10 A model for Performance Measurement

▽ the notion that many services have a target population
▽ the need for both producers and consumers to be involved in specifying
   service standards

Conclusion

It may be comforting to conclude that there are clear and simple solutions
to the many difficulties involved in developing performance measures, and
that there is a perfect set of measures just waiting to be discovered; but
this would be totally wrong. The task of defining performance and how it
should be measured is essentially a political process. New definitions emerge
from changes in party political philosophy and power, from the constantly
changing organizational power structure within local authorities and from
changes in public opinion. Definitions of performance and the relative
weight given to different performance measures result from the relative
power of the main stakeholders in the local government arena. If the 1980s
were dominated by the interests of those who were concerned with economy
and efficiency, there have been signs in the last few years of a significant
change of interest. In so far as the language of performance appears to be
dominated by one letter, it might be expected that the attention that has
been given to the three E's will now be redirected to the five A's: Accessi-
bility, Awareness, Accountability, Availability and Appropriateness.

Questions

▲ *What precise criteria are used to define the performance of individual services
   in your local authority?*
▲ *Try using Figures 4.9 and 4.10 to develop performance measures for a
   particular service.*
▲ *Define your own quality criteria for a service of which you are a customer.
   Are they measurable criteria?*
▲ *What external sources of comparison are used in your authority?*

5 Managing individual performance

Introduction

This chapter has a very broad title but a very specific purpose. In turning attention from organizational performance to individual performance the aim is to explore just one aspect of a broad subject – the use of formal schemes of *Performance Appraisal*. The case for adopting such a narrow focus rests on the importance which should now be attached to it. In the current climate and circumstances of local government, performance appraisal can no longer be considered an optional activity for local authorities.

The case for appraisal

The fundamental importance of appropriate schemes of performance appraisal has been stated so many times in recent years that it may appear unnecessary to restate it here. But it appears the message has not yet been fully received by some local authorities, who continue to debate its relevance and appropriateness. At the risk of repetition, therefore, performance appraisal is fundamentally necessary for three reasons:

▽ The staff of a local authority are its most expensive and important resource, and it is their activities, attitudes and behaviour, which are the main determinants of the performance of the local authority as a whole.
▽ For staff to perform well they must:
  – know clearly what is expected of them
  – be able to contribute to the process of defining those expectations
  – be motivated to perform well
  – have the opportunity and support necessary for improving their performance
  – be able to review their performance so that they can learn from their own experience and from the feedback they receive from others.
▽ The local authority must therefore have appropriate procedures for planning and appraising the activities and achievements of all staff, for ensuring that their potential is fulfilled and they are appropriately rewarded.

Performance appraisal should therefore seek to achieve mutual benefits for the local authority and for the individual employee. To be successful it is essential that it is seen both as an *organizational* event, necessary for the learning, development and success of the local authority, and as a *personal* event between two or more people whose working lives constantly interact with each other. The integration of organizational and personal requirements represents the key to designing and operating successful performance appraisal schemes. Success is also dependent on conceiving performance appraisal as a process of *learning* rather than as a process of direction and control. By using learning as the starting point for thinking, it is possible to emphasize certain characteristics of performance appraisal which are essential to any type of scheme which may be implemented. These are:

▽   that the process of learning is essential to all organizational and individual survival and development
▽   that in order to be of practical benefit to the organization, performance appraisal should be seen as an important way of learning not just – for the *appraisee* but also for the *appraiser* and also for the *organization* as a whole.

A recent history of performance appraisal

A 1986 survey by the Institute of Personnel Management indicated that there has been a substantial increase in the use of performance appraisal schemes in all kinds of organizations. That increase appears to have been substantially reflected in local government, with significant numbers of local authorities having adopted performance appraisal for the first time in recent years, and with many others adapting and improving their existing schemes. The reasons for the growth are many – certainly all of the general circumstances affecting local government, which were referred to in Chapter 1, are of relevance, but there are two additional issues which have helped promote the concept of appraisal:

▽   first, there has been an increased acceptance in local government of the need to relate remuneration directly to performance, particularly for senior management. The introduction of Performance Related Pay has necessitated, for the first time in some local authorities, the development of a clear process of appraisal as a basis for awarding remuneration.
▽   second, the changes in the power of trade unions, and a shift in their attitude towards performance appraisal, has meant that some local authorities have felt able to implement certain kinds of appraisal schemes which formerly they would have been reluctant to do, for fear of substantial opposition.

The increased use of performance appraisal is, therefore, like that of Performance Management more generally, part of a change in the climate and culture of local government. But it would be simplistic to suggest that performance appraisal can be implemented easily, or that its past history has been entirely satisfactory.

The history of performance appraisal has, in some local authorities, been an unproductive one, with a life cycle (not unlike that of some

Performance Review Sub-Committees) of only two to three years, during which time a scheme is designed, never fully implemented and supported, and gradually withers away as a result of direct opposition, or of simple neglect, or because it did not produce the performance results anticipated. In some cases such schemes are not entirely abandoned but remain in use, in an adapted form, in one or two departments. For example, Leicester City Council carried out an analysis of staff development in 1989 which revealed that six different appraisal schemes were operating in different departments. The impact of such departmentalized schemes on an authority as a whole tends to be marginal.

The examples of the rather mixed success of performance appraisal provide a rich vein of information from which can be drawn the following reasons for its failure in the past:

▽ problems relating to their strategy, objectives and clarity of purpose
▽ problems relating to the mechanisms or processes of the schemes
▽ problems relating to the attitudes, styles and skills of appraisers and appraisees.

Strategy, objectives and clarity of purpose

Past experience suggests that the most important determinant of success is the extent to which any proposed scheme is set appropriately within the context of the prevailing philosophy and management culture of the local authority – or, where change is considered to be necessary – is introduced as an integral part of a strategic approach to changing the managerial philosophy and culture. In other words, *a scheme of performance appraisal must embody the existing or intended culture of the local authority.* In order to adopt a strategic approach of performance appraisal it is of course necessary for senior management to have a clear, articulated view of what the actual or intended philosophy and culture of the local authority is. In the past such a view has often been significantly lacking, and its absence has had a marked influence on the failure of many schemes. Increasingly however, in a number of local authorities, councillors and senior managers have developed a more strategic approach and have ensured that it is communicated throughout the local authority, thereby significantly increasing the likelihood of appropriate and successful schemes being designed.

Even where there is a clear understanding of the strategic relationship between organizational culture and performance appraisal it is still important that the precise objectives of the scheme are made clear. Performance appraisal has been introduced with a wide variety of objectives, as can be seen from Figure 5.1, some of which may be mutually incompatible. As a result some schemes may have contradictions and dichotomies built into them which lead to inevitable problems when they are implemented. The most common contradictions are:

▽ the extent to which the scheme is intended to encourage and support a *competitive* or *cooperative* culture

* To identify employee strengths and weaknesses.
* To develop/train employees in their present jobs.
* To identify individuals for promotion.
* To plan career progression.
* To recognize good work.
* To provide a basis for salary progression/performance-related pay.
* To establish and monitor performance objectives and targets.
* To clarify accountabilities and responsibilities.
* To alert managers to constraints which inhibit employee performance.
* To encourage/require managers to manage their staff in a systematic way.
* To develop communication between managers and their staff.
* To help develop a participative environment.
* To improve employee job satisfaction and motivation.
* To ensure equity in the treatment of employees.
* To encourage self-evaluation.

Figure 5.1 Examples of Objectives of Performance Appraisal Schemes

▽ the extent to which the scheme is concerned with *rewarding* or *punishing* appraisees
▽ the extent to which the scheme is intending to encourage and support a *participative* or a *directive* culture.

The mechanisms and processes of performance appraisal

Schemes of performance appraisal have to be carefully designed. They require a shape and a structure which must be defined in terms of such matters as:

▽ the frequency of appraisal
▽ the criteria of appraisal
▽ the format and content of the appraisal itself
▽ procedures for resolving disagreements between appraiser and appraisee
▽ the format for recording the results of appraisal
▽ arrangements for monitoring the introduction and implementation of the scheme and for sustaining it over time.

Designing performance appraisal schemes is not an excessively difficult task, particularly where there is a clear strategy and set of objectives to work to, but it does have to be undertaken with care. Recent experience suggests that a number of problems can arise in the procedures, the most important of which are as follows:

▽ a lack of reliability, validity and relevance in the criteria and measures used in the appraisal. Where specific targets are used within the appraisal process it is particularly important to ensure that they relate a) to the most significant part of the appraisee's job; b) to quality as well as quantity and cost of work performed on results achieved.
▽ over-dependence on subjective evaluation, with little or no attempt to create objective criteria, benchmarks or targets. The aim should be to create an appropriate balance between objectivity and subjectivity, for objective measures and targets can never entirely replace the need for subjective evaluation, nor should this be attempted. But the reliance on subjective evaluation can often be simply a way of avoiding the

necessary but sometimes difficult task of identifying and developing appropriate objective measures and targets.

▽ feedback is often too remote from performance. If the annual appraisal interview is perceived and used as the *only* opportunity to give feedback, it is likely that the precise details and circumstances being appraised may have been partly forgotten or will have already been 'rationalized-away' by the appraisee and the feedback therefore ignored. The appraisal interview should not therefore replace the practice of giving feedback regularly as part of the day-to-day managerial and supervisory process – it merely supplements it by providing a formal opportunity and space for more in-depth appraisal.

The attitudes, styles and skills needed for appraisal

Experience suggests that developing appropriate attitudes, styles and skills is fundamental to the success of performance appraisal schemes, but that in practice insufficient attention has been given to these aspects of implementation. Training in skill development and in the operation of a scheme is also essential and can go some way to overcoming the problems which will inevitably arise. But ultimately success will depend on the scheme being set within a clear managerial and service philosophy which is clearly expressed and constantly reiterated and reinforced. The performance appraisal scheme itself will also need constant monitoring and support if it is not to wither away.

However well designed a scheme, certain problems are almost certain to arise and therefore need particular attention.

Appraisees – a proportion of appraisees will be reluctant to open themselves to appraisal and evaluation – they may not see this as a valid route to improving their own performance. Appraisers will need guidance on how to deal positively with the 'closed', unresponsive employee.

Appraisees and Appraisers may be unwilling or unable to recognize and explore those aspects of the appraisee's performance which are influenced by or conditional upon the performance of the appraiser. In any line management situation there is inevitably an area of 'joint performance' where the superior affects the performance of the subordinate and vice versa. This can be of vital importance to their overall performance but is an area which requires the development of considerable skill if it is to be handled constructively for both parties.

Appraisers – a proportion of appraisers will dislike doing formal appraisals and as a consequence are likely to do them badly or, if given the opportunity, not at all. Appraisers may also err on the side either of being excessively authoritarian, directive and negatively critical (thereby demotivating appraisees and providing little incentive for them to involve themselves positively in the scheme) or, of being excessively permissive, non-directive and congratulatory (with the result that appraisees end up setting their own objectives and performance targets and receive little or no feedback or appraisal of their performance). Striking the balance is again a matter of style and skill which can in large part be taught to, and developed by, individual appraisers.

But perhaps the most problematic area is the degree of inaccuracy which may be exhibited by appraisers when making evaluations and rating performance. Inaccurate assessments naturally create feelings of injustice and quickly lead to a deterioration in the perceived value of the scheme. There is however ample evidence that appraisers consistently make errors when rating performance. ACAS, the Advisory, Conciliation and Arbitration Service, have helpfully summarized some of the main types of errors made, in their occasional paper by Graham James (1988). He identifies the following:

▽ the halo effect: where rating in one quality or area influences ratings in other qualities or areas.

▽ the leniency/severity effect: the general tendency to assign extreme ratings.

▽ the contrast effect: the tendency to rate an individual in relation to other employees rather than on the requirements of his/her job.

▽ the similarity affect: the tendency to rate an individual according to how the appraiser views that individual in relation to him/herself – hence greater similarity produces higher ratings.

▽ the error of central tendency: the tendency to rate all individuals in the middle of the scale because it is a 'safe' rating. This is a particularly common error which some schemes try to overcome by having no mid-point – i.e. they use, for example, a four-point scale. However, while such scales overcome some of the problems of central tendency, they create difficulties in rating individuals whose performance is properly described as satisfactory or adequate.

▽ the first impression error: the tendency for initial evaluations to over-shadow subsequent performance.

▽ the recency error: the tendency for performance achievements in the immediate past to be given a greater weighting than earlier achievements.

▽ overdependence on a single source: the tendency to generalize on the basis of one or two behavioural cues or a very limited number of objective measures or targets which do not cover the whole of an individual's job.

▽ cognitive errors: which may relate either to the memory limitations of appraisers or to their inability to collect adequate information about an appraisee's performance.

▽ causal attributions: the way in which an appraiser tends to explain the causes of good or bad performance can significantly affect assessments. Causal attributions may be either *external* (i.e. the situational or circumstantial factors which influence or determine an individual's performance) or *internal* (i.e. the characteristics, abilities and skills of the individual which influence or determine his/her performance).

▽ stereotyping: the use of over-simplified, over-generalized and sometimes inaccurate descriptions of particular groups in society which then influence the assessment made of individuals who belong to those groups.

Equal opportunities and appraisal

The last two assessment and rating errors, causal attributions and stereotyping, are particularly relevant to the impact on equal opportunities of performance appraisal schemes. Because of the structure of employment in local authority departments the majority of appraisers will be white, male managers. Where they hold stereotypical or prejudicial attitudes towards their female, black or disabled staff, or indeed towards any identifiable group of staff, it is likely that their assessments will be excessively biased – either negatively or positively. For example the ACAS working paper refers to research which has demonstrated that prejudiced male managers are more likely to attribute good performance by their female staff to external factors such as luck or the simplicity of the task, whereas unprejudiced managers are more likely to attribute that performance to internal factors such as the abilities and characteristics of the female staff. Stereotyping is likely to lead to bias in the form of prejudging performance without direct consideration of the facts or to excessive leniency or severity in assessment.

Apart from bias in assessment it is also important to be aware of the cultural assumptions on which performance appraisals are based. The assumption that direct face-to-face discussion, analysis and assessment is a positive, acceptable and normal form of social interaction may be culturally bound – that is, it may not be accepted in all cultures. While it is necessary for any performance appraisal scheme to be based on the assumptions of a majority culture, it is important that appraisers when carrying out appraisals make themselves sympathetically aware of any different cultural assumptions which may be held by their appraisees and adapt their approach accordingly.

Directness v indirectness

Considerations of cultural assumptions give rise to a more subtle difficulty. Built into the concept of performance appraisal is an assumption that both feedback and appraisal should be direct (face-to-face) and be based on clear objectives, criteria and measures (to create a sense of clarity, fairness and precision). Both these characteristics are necessary and important – but both can be taken to extremes. They can result in an authoritarian, didactic, blunt process of 'telling' people, particularly in relation to the poorer aspects of their performance. Stress may easily be laid on a one-way process where clarity, precision and direction are imposed rather than agreed.

In an appraisal interview that equality of opportunity may not exist and it can become a blunt and painful experience. At the other extreme, where appraisers find it difficult to conduct face-to-face appraisal, whether for cultural or psychological reasons, they will veer in the opposite direction by avoiding any attempt to ensure that the interview has a truly evaluative component. This may be less directly harmful but is unlikely to produce positive results.

Performance appraisal as a learning process

There is a difference between *telling* somebody that they are not (or are) performing well (i.e. an evaluation which is external to the individual – carried out by somebody else with reference to them) and creating the *opportunity for self-evaluation*. Telling – particularly when backed by power or coercion – can frequently produce impressive short-term improvements in performance. In the long-term however it may not be so impressive, leading to disputes, avoidance and game-playing (i.e. attempting to fix the criteria or measures of performance in favour of the appraisee without reference to broader organizational objectives or purpose) and eventually to a reduction in performance. Most importantly, it is unlikely to produce a situation where appraisees perform to their full potential or ability, for to achieve this requires that they internalize, accept and evaluate themselves against a set of agreed performance criteria. In psychological terms it represents the difference between theories of behaviour modification and self-motivated learning. For individuals to effect long-term and continuous improvement or maintenance of their performance they must themselves be motivated so to do. The appraisal process can encourage that process if it is seen essentially as a process of *learning* in which appraisee and appraiser momentarily pause from the hurly-burly of everyday activity in order to:

▽ reflect on past performance
▽ evaluate that performance
▽ identify solutions and make decisions about future performance
▽ decide on how the solutions/decisions can be acted upon.

Each stage is equally important – they represent the four main stages in the process of learning. But it is not easy to create that balance within an interview process – there is always a tendency (created by either circumstances or personal prediliction) to give undue weight to one aspect at the expense of others.

Considering performance appraisal as a process of learning is important not only from the individual appraisee's point of view but also from that of the appraiser and the organization as a whole. For successful appraisal to take place it is essential that the appraiser also sees him/herself engaged eventually in a process of learning – which may involve finding answers to questions such as:

▽ how is the appraisee's performance contributing to organization objectives?
▽ what motivates him/her?
▽ how does my style/approach to managing him/her affect motivation and performance?
▽ what circumstances are contributing (positively or negatively) to the appraisee's performance?

The process of learning needs to permeate the whole organization for it to be fully effective – which is why it is so important that a scheme of perform-ance appraisal must cover all employees and not just some. It is by so doing that ultimately an organization can learn about its performance by addressing questions such as:

▽ how are policies being implemented in practice?
▽ what circumstances are helping/hindering our staff with regard to the successful implemation of our policies?
▽ what can be done to create the conditions which best motivate staff to perform to a high standard?

A performance appraisal scheme is not, of course, the only mechanism for creating an organization which learns, and by learning, achieves. It is just one.

The importance of having a formal scheme

> Good managers don't need formal schemes for performance appraisal – they appraise continuously as a natural and integral part of their work. Bad managers need formal schemes but are likely to implement them badly.

This statement can be used as a reason for not having a formal scheme, but it should not, for it is a statement which can be applied to every aspect of organizational life – not just to appraisal. In a perfect organization with perfect people, very little formalization of management procedures might be necessary. But neither people nor organizations are perfect and as a consequence it becomes necessary to formalize and structure the aspects of organizational life which are considered to be vital to the survival, health and achievement of the organization and its members. That does not mean that everything need be formalized, nor that each organization will need to formalize the same things in the same way – formalization will vary according to what is perceived as important and vital in each case.

Local authorities, because of the circumstances they face, their com-plexity, the size and importance of their human resources, and because of the importance of accountability, must provide some degree of formaliz-ation in their procedures for appraising individuals – they have no choice. The area of choice they do have is in the precise objectives, type and style of formal scheme they adopt.

The main types of performance appraisal schemes

Although schemes vary widely in their objectives and procedures they can generally be grouped into three broad categories.

1 Developmental schemes

Frequently referred to as 'staff development', these schemes focus on the developmental and training needs of individuals. They seek to match the expectations and aspirations of the employee to the staffing needs of the organization so as to realize the potential of human resources. The

appraisal interviews carried out in these schemes will typically have five
elements:

▽ a review of the job content and role of the appraisee
▽ an analysis of the skills, abilities and competencies needed by the
   appraisee to fulfil their job satisfactorily
▽ a review of the personal plans and aspirations of the appraisee
▽ the identification of developmental and training needs including possible modifications to the appraisee's role and job
▽ specification of an action plan to put (iv) into effect.

Such schemes grew in popularity during the 1970's and early 1980's princi-
pally because they were perceived to be appropriate for that time, their
approach to performance being relatively low key. They were also the type
of scheme for which trade union agreement could be obtained, as they
were perceived as least threatening to staff. Some schemes had little effect,
being poorly implemented with little support and training for those
involved.

2 Performance improvement schemes

Based on a process of ensuring that individuals and their managers
achieve precise understanding and agreement as to what is expected of
each employee, and that continuous improvements in performance are
achieved, these schemes need to be closely linked to the procedures for
determining organization performance. They have the following elements:

▽ Defining job accountabilities or responsibilities
▽ Setting and agreeing performance objectives and targets
▽ Appraising performance against targets on an annual or six-monthly
   basis
▽ Identifying significant constraints on, and obstacles to, satisfactory or
   improved performance, and agreeing ways of overcoming them.

This type of scheme has become increasingly popular in local government
and often forms the starting point for the development of reward-based
appraisal schemes. They have, as a consequence, been developed and
improved beyond the simple four-stage process outlined above and their
introduction to local authorities has often been carried out by private sector
management consultants.

3 Reward based appraisal schemes

Schemes of this type are concerned with appraising performance as a
basis for allocating different kinds of rewards. There are three main sub-
divisions.

A. SCHEMES FOR PROMOTION AND REGRADING

Most local authorities have some form of assessment review for new
recruits. The importance and value attached to them varies greatly depend-

ing on the degree to which they have become a routinized part of the bureaucratic procedures for staff recruitment. Some local authorities use them in an analytical and supportive way which goes beyond simply assessing an individual's suitability for continuing employment and involves the identification of issues in which new employees may need counselling and training.

Many local authorities have also developed Career Grades covering three or four salary grades, progression through which is dependent on successful assessments. Schemes of this kind tend to be departmentally based. They are common, for example, in Social Services departments and are used with some success to relate remuneration to performance and experience. Their limitations arise in situations where employee performance is not otherwise explicitly assessed and there is no culture of appraisal. This can result in situations where neither appraisee nor appraiser are clear as to the criteria to be used nor how any criteria are to be applied. They can also produce the classic problem of reward-based appraisals – the conflict of basic objectives between the appraisee, whose objective is reward, and the appraiser, whose objective is performance. It is widely accepted that having reward as the focal point of a performance appraisal interview is not a good idea. Additional remuneration should be regarded as a reward for good performance rather than the reason for having the interview.

B. BONUS INCENTIVE SCHEMES

Bonus schemes for manual workers fell into some disrepute by the 1970's but, as Alan Fowler (1988) notes:

> While many local authorities have abandoned the conventional work-study based individual incentive schemes which had been developed in the 1960's, they have not all abandoned the concept of incentives generally.

Indeed it may be argued that the use of incentives has increased, particularly in D.L.O's and D.S.O's, where the use of group-based bonus schemes based on financial performance is increasingly common. Fowler also identifies that in other areas of work there has been a movement towards converting individually-paid bonus schemes to group-based ones which use the concept of measured day-work to set staffing levels in relation to outputs of specified quantity and quality.

Opportunities for local authorities to extend the use of bonus schemes based on financial measures of performance are created by the increased use of contract management and the use of service level agreements. However, while contractual principles are likely to greatly extend the type and range of activities for which financial measure of performance can be devised, it is unlikely that this can be done for all areas of local authority activity. There is therefore a danger of developing a sense of inequality between different groups of staff, as has already occurred in some local authorities which have, as a result, blocked initiatives by certain groups of staff to move to incentive-based remuneration.

The movement towards group-based incentives is highly relevant to the future of performance-related pay schemes. Many local authority departments lay emphasis on a team-based culture as a general principle and there are many activities and services which of their nature require a team approach. Individually-based incentive schemes run counter to a team ethos and can be a source of divisiveness.

C. PERFORMANCE RELATED PAY SCHEMES

These schemes, which are most frequently introduced at senior management level and are individually based, are discussed later in this chapter.

A practical approach to performance appraisal

The introduction of a performance appraisal scheme, whether or not it is incentive-based, requires careful planning. While generalized advice always requires local interpretation, there are a number of general design considerations which apply to most situations.

1 Strategy and objectives

▽ What is the predominant culture of the authority – autocratic, benevolent, consultative, competitive or participative? The question is often difficult to answer because most local authorities contain elements of all five. That, however, may be a problem which needs to be confronted.
▽ What culture and style do you want to create, and what part can an appraisal play in the achievement of change?
▽ How will an appraisal scheme link with other human resource processes such as recruitment, disciplinary procedures and training programmes? There is, for example, little point in introducing a scheme focused on development and training if you do not have adequate training capability and resources.
▽ What are your specific objectives – in this chapter amongst those identified earlier?
▽ How will the scheme be introduced – comprehensively, gradually or as a pilot? Pilot schemes can be a useful way of refining and designing-out problems but they can also signify a lack of widespread agreement as to the purpose of, or need for, a scheme.
▽ What levels of staff will it apply to? It is rarely possible to design a uniform scheme which will work for all types and levels of employee. Some authorities have designed schemes which consist of an overall framework which can be adapted to individual circumstances by, for example, varying the criteria for assessing performance.

2 The design of the system

Schemes will vary considerably in their precise characteristics and procedures. There are however certain elements which should be common to all schemes.

CLARIFYING RESPONSIBILITIES AND ACCOUNTABILITIES

Job descriptions do not always make clear the purpose(s) for which a job exists whereas statements of principle responsibilities and accountabilities can provide that clarity. It is generally accepted that responsibilities are 'timeless' and therefore unlikely to change from year to year but they may have some priority attached to them which can change. Examples of the main headings used to describe responsibilities and accountabilities of chief executives are illustrated in Figure 5.2.

I   *STRATEGY* – To assist members to formulate clear objectives and affordable programmes for the development of the Borough and the services for which the Council is responsible having regard to changing political priorities, statutory provisions and community needs and expectations.

II   *DIRECTION* – To give clear direction to the organization by producing and communicating achievable operational plans which reflect the Council's policy and spending decisions and agreed organizational goals.

III   *IMPLEMENTATION* – To provide the full range of agreed services to the specified standards and within approved budgets, to deliver capital schemes on time and within authorized cost limits and to achieve other agreed policy objectives and organizational goals to acceptable standards and agreed timescales.

IV   *ORGANIZATIONAL   CONTROL AND DEVELOPMENT* – To enable the Council to function as a cost-effective public body by ensuring that its structures and processes meet the needs of a democratically controlled body and that the working environment and working methods are continually reviewed and updated to reflect best practice elsewhere in the public sector, and, where appropriate – in the private sector.

V   *STAFF   MANAGEMENT   AND DEVELOPMENT* – To recruit, direct, supervise and develop subordinate managers and to make arrangements for the training and development of all staff to meet the requirements of their current jobs and to prepare for new challenges and opportunities.

VI   *PERSONAL EFFECTIVENESS* – To develop, maintain and use the full range of knowledge and skills in order to be effective in all accountabilities, to assist Members in the effective government of the Borough and to promote Bexley as an efficient unit of local government.

1:   *Leadership*
Ensure the visibility of the office of Chief Executive as the central force for leading and co-ordinating the Council's staff.

2:   *Policy Advice*
Provide sound information and advice for the Council to make policy decisions, so that members are aware of the availability of resources and of the competing demands for them.

3:   *Management Systems*
Advise the Council on the systematic control and management of its activities, to ensure efficient and effective responses to the Council's instructions.

4:   *Implementation*
Lead the Directors, and monitor their performance, so as to achieve the Council's stated objectives.

5:   *Resources*
Ensure the creative management of the three major resources of people, finance and property, in order to enhance the Council's ability to meet its objectives.

6:   *Corporate Management*
Develop corporate working across all departments, in order to create and implement a corporate strategy.

7:   *Communication*
a) Ensure effective communication within the Authority about the Council's objectives, to create a sense of purpose and promote and sustain a high level of morale in staff.
b) Communicate the Council's activities externally, so as to promote public understanding of the Council's achievements and current dilemmas.

Figure 5.2 Examples of Accountabilities of Chief Executives

The principal responsibilities of individuals cannot always be identified in isolation. In organizations where there is no clear framework which identifies where responsibility lies for which decisions, it may be necessary to undertake a responsibility-mapping exercise to identify levels of authority, responsibilities and inter-relationships.

IDENTIFYING KEY TASKS AND TARGETS

The language used in this part of the appraisal process varies enormously – key tasks, key management tasks, objectives, performance standards, targets and measures all being terms used. The extent to which key tasks and targets are identified in detail also varies, being dependent on the scheme's orientation towards either personal development or towards the achievement of specific results. Schemes of the latter type are usually concerned with achieving precision and specificity in the definition of targets and measures, and the issues that arise are similar to those discussed in Chapter 4, particularly with regard to the problem of achieving a balance between quantitive and qualitative assessment. Many of the schemes introduced with the help of consultants in recent years have sought to achieve high levels of measurability. That objective has been beneficial in those situations where little or no target-setting or measurement of results had previously existed, but the process can become obsessional, with the result that short-term measurable achievements dominate the appraisal process.

Managing performance does however require that a mutually agreed set of expectations is stated as precisely as possible. Key tasks and targets can be used very successfully to stimulate and motivate staff to make improvements in their performance and changes in their behaviour, but there are a number of factors which will determine the extent to which that success can be achieved:

▽ Are the targets realistic? Are they perceived as achievable?
▽ Are the targets challenging and stretching or can they be achieved without effort?
▽ How are the targets determined? Are they imposed from above, or determined from below, or negotiated?
▽ Do the targets express a concern for quality as well as quantity?
▽ Do the targets motivate staff to concentrate on the most important aspects of their jobs?
▽ Is the achievement of the target within the control of the appraisee or is he/she dependent on others? If the latter is the case consideration should be given to using group targets or to co-ordinating the target-setting exercise for all those involved.
▽ Can short-term targets be adequately linked to the achievements of long-term goals?

ACTION PLANNING

The process is completed by writing statements of the actions needing to be taken to achieve the defined targets or objectives, together with some reference to the assumptions on which the plan is based and any constraints which may influence its achievement.

APPRAISING

The heart of the appraisal process is the appraisal interview, which in most schemes occurs annually, but may sometimes also include a half-yearly review. They come in many shapes and sizes and much has been written about how they can best be conducted. Justice cannot be done here to that body of knowledge but, briefly, it is possible to identify the following key issues:

▽ *Planning* and preparation by both appraiser and appraisee is essential.
▽ *Purpose* must be mutually clear. Appraisals may be thought of as 'conversations with a purpose'.
▽ *Timing* and *Sequence* of the interview are vital.
▽ *Adaptability* is essential, for there is no single best way to conduct an interview.
▽ *Learning* and *Problem-Solving* should be the fundamental characteristics of the interview.

Interviews need to be supported by sufficient documentation to ensure that the appraisal process is properly planned and is implemented equitably and consistently. 'Sufficient' in this context should be interpreted as 'the necessary minimum', for schemes can become more of a form-filling chore than a process of inter-personal communication. Explanatory pamphlets, written for appraisees and appraisers, contribute greatly to the success of appraisal by creating mutual clarity and understanding for all who are involved in the process.

Training is the sine qua non of all successful appraisal, and the skills of appraisal interviewing can have an impact on the conduct of inter-personal relationships which spreads far wider than the formal appraisal process.

Confirmation and countersigning

The majority of schemes which involve making a specific assessment of the appraisee will normally include a role for a confirming or countersigning officer who may have a number of functions, the most important of which are to ensure that the appraisal scheme is being implemented fully and fairly, and to act as an arbitrator in the event of unresolved disputes between appraisers and appraisees. In ensuring that the appraisal process is being fully implemented it is important that he or she acts as a role-model for the process by fully discussing any significant issues which arise in the appraisal forms with the appraiser and, when necessary, the appraisee. The need for equity and fairness arises in two ways. First there is the need to ensure consistency in the standard of the assessments made by different appraisers and second, in view of the comments made earlier about the sources of bias in the appraisal process, it is important that he or she should identify any discriminatory practices which occur and then intervene in order to prevent them.

The role of a confirming or countersigning appraiser is an important one but can easily become regarded as reduced to a routine chore, thereby reducing the significance of the appraisal process.

Team based appraisal

The great majority of schemes in the public and private sectors are based on a one-to-one relationship between appraisee and appraiser. The focus of such schemes is on individual performance and the manager-subordinate relationship. But in many situations, performance can be seen as the product of group or team activity, and the achievement of high levels of performance is as dependent on the ability of the team to work cohesively as it is on the skills and abilities of its individual members. In other words, the sum is greater than the parts. Advocates of individual performance appraisal tend to argue that, even where team working is important, a well structured system of individual goals and targets should be capable of identifying and reflecting the contributions which every member of a team must make if it is to perform well. This argument has some merits, but its weakness lies in the fact that, if the process of setting goals and targets is an individual one, it is less likely to incorporate a full consideration of the contribution to performance made as a result of team activity. In addition, it fails to recognize the importance which needs to be placed on involving the team in setting its goals and targets. Team commitment to goals and targets is as important as individual commitment.

In organizations where team working is an important characteristic of the workplace, and where it is therefore important to build a strong team ethos, there is a strong case for team- or group-based appraisal schemes. Some local authorities, of which Dorset County Council is an example, are beginning to recognize the importance of such schemes, which they are now implementing. Perhaps the most important characteristic of schemes of this type is that they may be seen as a means for undertaking team development as well as appraisal, and therefore become an integral part of the broader process of management.

Team-based systems can be designed in a variety of ways, although it is usual for each team to contain its manager. The identification of objectives and targets is then carried out as a team task under the guidance of the manager. Appraisals of performance may then be carried out regularly as part of the normal working environment, but may be supplemented by individual appraisals in some cases.

The potential benefit of team-based schemes is considerable, particularly where they become an integral part of the team's approach to its tasks. The effect of possible bias in assessment can be reduced, and judgements based on consensus can be more readily accepted, and therefore have greater impact on the individuals in the group. But most importantly, a team approach may form an essential element in building a co-operative culture within the organization.

Performance related pay schemes (PRP)

Perhaps the most significant development in the area of performance management has been the introduction of PRP for senior managers in local
authorities. With many schemes now in operation or being considered, it
is interesting to note that as recently as 1985 Butt and Palmer were able
to report that . . . 'At management level we have seen little evidence of
such schemes'. PRP is significant not only for the extent and speed of its
implementation, but also for the fact that it represents a major move away
from traditional patterns of thinking about remuneration. Before turning
to the details of how PRP schemes operate, it is important to reflect on
these changes and their broader significance for the management of local
government.

The incentives culture gap

There has been a cultural gap between the public and private sectors
with regard to providing performance incentives. That gap remains in a
number of local authorities where the language of incentives remains an
object of suspicion. This originates partly from their experience of bonus
incentive schemes for manual workers in the 1960's and 1970's but, more
significantly, results from an essentially bureaucratic view of performance
in which individuals are perceived as having a defined job to do. Taking
this view, performance is defined by a job description or role definition,
supplemented by self-motivating professionalism and an ethos of public
service, and backed up by hierarchical authority and control. With this
view of performance, incentives are irrelevant and unnecessary.

Increasingly, however, there has been a readiness to acknowledge, as
has been done much more openly in the private sector, that individuals,
groups and organizations will perform better if they are provided with
appropriate and direct incentives. In this view of performance there is a
basic assumption that if individuals and groups can increase (or decrease)
their personal rewards directly as a result of the decisions they make and
the actions they undertake, then their performance, however described,
will improve.

The breakout from national pay scales

The introduction of PRP is only one manifestation of a much broader
movement away from the traditional nationally-agreed structure of pay and
conditions towards the creation of locally-determined schemes. During the
1980's it became increasingly recognized that the national system formed
a stranglehold on local authorities. The principal perceived problems were:

▽   that the narrow salary ranges within the national system created prob-
     lems of inflexibility and lack of incentive.
▽   that a system which provided for individuals to progress automatically
     through the increments in a pay scale, without reference to performance
     or achievement, created a situation where there was little or no relation-

ship between performance and pay, thus being inequitable and providing little motivation or incentive to improve performance.

▽ the increasing difficulties experienced by some local authorities in
recruiting and retaining staff. This was in part a geographical problem,
resulting from highly differential regional rates of employment and
house prices which, in a society increasingly dependent on home owner-
ship, effectively precluded the movement of potential employees into
certain regions of the country, particularly London and South-East
England.

The difficulties were also caused by a changing employment market nation-
ally and regionally, which resulted in particular difficulties in recruiting
skilled and professional staff for whose services local authorities were in
competition with the private sector. The groups involved included not only
professional staff such as lawyers, engineers and accountants, but also
skilled non-professionals such as computer staff, and manual tradesmen
such as plumbers, who could command higher remuneration in the private
sector. The problem was aggravated by the introduction of Compulsory
Competitive Tendering, which resulted in private sector firms actively and
successfully recruiting local authority managers to help them compete for
local authority contracts.

Some local authorities responded to these problems by making relatively minor adjustments – by, for example, combining two or three con-
ventional grades, or by providing additional local increments to the conven-
tional grades. Recruitment problems have also been addressed by providing
an enhanced range of relocation benefits, which include mortgage subsidies
and housing equity sharing schemes. Local authorities have also attempted
to match a private sector practice by providing a range of other benefits
which include car leasing, private health insurance and life insurance.
Within DLO's there have also been examples of the use of a variety of
bonus and profit-sharing schemes.

But other local authorities, perhaps encouraged by the government's
attitude towards national pay bargaining, and influenced by the prevailing
climate of escalating remuneration levels for senior managers in the private
sector, adopted the more radical solution of introducing Performance
Related Pay based, in a number of cases, on broadly determined pay bands
and term contracts.

The concern with recruitment and retention problems is central to the
kind of PRP schemes which are being introduced in local government. It
is now clear that local authorities have had two quite different objectives
in introducing PRP. On the one hand there are those authorities whose
primary objective has been to improve their performance and regard PRP
as a way of providing the necessary conditions and incentives for senior
managers to achieve this. On the other hand there are those local authorities
whose primary objective has been to provide a pay package designed to
improve the recruitment and retention of senior staff. Of this latter group
of local authorities, LACSAB, who have carried out the most detailed
investigation into PRP in local government yet undertaken, and whose
work is referred to extensively in the remainder of this chapter, make quite
clear that in their view the use of PRP to improve recruitment and retention

is unlikely to create long term benefits, and may even produce major difficulties:

> If, however, the flexibility that PRP creates is also used to tackle other issues (for example recruitment and retention of scarce skills or responding to regional variations in pay), the robust criteria required for specifying good performance will be weakened by non-performance considerations. Such mixed objectives will make it more, not less, difficult to get pay decisions right. It will weaken focus on performance and employees will question whether the organization genuinely values or fairly rewards good performance. Any motivational effect that PRP can have will eventually be lost. An organization misusing PRP in this way is likely in time to see its salary bill rise without getting any return in higher performance. Examples of this phenomenon are the slack approaches to payments by results and productivity bargaining in the last two decades.
> (LACSAB: Handbook on Performance Related Pay 1990. p. 8.)

The last sentence of the quotation is important in so far as it is noticeable that, while moving away from productivity bargaining for more junior staff, and especially manual workers, it is perhaps surprising to find some local authorities so ready to adopt the same principle for its most senior staff. While there are clearly differences between the characteristics of the jobs performed by senior managers and manual workers which may make some form of performance- or productivity-related reward appropriate to the former and not to the latter, the reverse may equally well be argued, for it is undoubtedly more difficult to measure the output or achievement of senior managers than it is for manual workers. Performance-based payments are therefore less likely to be an accurate and equitable reflection of the true value of their performance to the organization than for manual workers. Is this therefore a case of: what was not good for the goose is now great for the gander? From a critical stance it may be argued that a few local authorities have simply reflected private sector practice by substantially increasing the remuneration and rewards of senior executives while tightly holding down those of shop-floor workers – the long-term consequences of which are highly uncertain.

Such criticisms cannot generally be levelled at those PRP schemes that are clearly aimed at providing an incentive for improving performance, and it is these schemes which are used as examples later in this chapter. This does not mean that they are perfect or free from problems, but they are more likely to have been carefully designed and to exist within local authorities which have a clearer and more consistent culture of performance-oriented management. It is not surprising therefore to find that some schemes of this kind are already being developed and improved by, for example, extending the scheme to lower grades of employees or by articulating improved criteria on which to base performance ratings.

A cautionary note

While few councillors and officers in local government would dispute the need for a performance-focused style and system of management, many are much more cautious about directly linking individual performance to pay. They have the right to be cautious, for a variety of reasons.

First, there has been very little objective evaluation of the consequences of PRP in local government. Whether it really improves performance is as much a matter of belief and subjective observation as of objective evaluation. However, in so far as belief is an important determinant of action, it is important to note that the LACSAB report of 18 case studies of PRP concludes:

> that in most of the case study organisations there was a firm belief that PRP was paying dividends and that the gains outweighed the disadvantages. The capacity of the more sophisticated performance review systems to clarify work objectives and integrate activities better at different levels of the organisation was particularly noteworthy.
> (LACSAB 'PRP in Practice' Case Studies from Local Government (1990) p. 4)

Given the increasing numbers of local authorities turning to PRP, there is an urgent need for an objective evaluation of its effects on performance, but there is a danger that senior managers, who have been the main beneficiaries of such schemes, may be in no hurry to instigate or support such an evaluation. It should also be noted that at a time when local government is moving towards PRP some private sector firms are abandoning it. Their analysis suggests that PRP, because of its proper tendency to focus on 'hard results' which can be objectively measured and rated, causes managers to give excessive attention to activities which produce short-term results at the expense of activities which may not have an immediate pay-off but which are nonetheless essential to the long term development, growth or survival of the firm. They have also found that the excessive focus on rewarding individual achievement is inappropriate to all working situations. Secondly, largely because the assessment of the value of PRP lies predominately in the area of belief rather than objective evaluation, it creates the conditions in which beliefs, both for and against it, can be strongly held and can result in considerable divisiveness and conflict within an organization. This is demonstrated by LACSAB in its reporting of the arguments presented for and against PRP (see Figure 5.3). The potential for conflict results not only from its impact on firmly-held beliefs, but also from the fact that the majority of schemes create a divide between those staff who are included and those who are excluded.

ARGUMENTS FOR AND AGAINST PERFORMANCE RELATED PAY

FOR	AGAINST
It's fair – it provides a framework for recognizing and rewarding individual's work.	It's unfair – it relies on subjective judgements which can be wrong.
It motivates – it encourages people to pursue high standards in the knowledge they will be rewarded.	It demotivates – for those who believe they will never get the extra payments.
It improves understanding between managers and their staff.	It destroys team spirit.
It increases performance and helps produce a performance culture.	It's distasteful and it complicates managers' jobs.
It helps focus resources in areas where they are most needed.	It's bureaucratic and costly.
It increases control over paybill costs.	It can lead to pay rising faster than performance.

Figure 5.3
(Adapted from: LACSAB Handbook on Performance Related Pay 1990)

Thirdly, the psychological basis which underpins the use of individual rewards and incentives has not been extensively explored in the managerial context. The theoretical basis for performance-based pay has been economic rather than psychological. It assumes that all individuals will seek to maximize their personal benefit. Organizations also seek to maximize their economic success, and performance-related pay operates at the interface between these two economic aims, providing a way of relating individual and organizational benefit. But whether individual psychology operates in the way assumed by economic theory is questionable. Moreover, because a local authority's primary objectives cannot be expressed purely in terms of economic success, it is unclear how economic rewards can be precisely related to a range of political goals.

In summary there are a number of questions which are as yet not clearly answered.

▽ Do rewards (in the form of incremental additions to pay) have the effect they are supposed to – i.e. do individuals respond in the way required and expected by working harder, better and more effectively in the pursuit of organizational goals?
▽ Do rewards continue to have a long-term as well as short-term effect?
▽ Do the specific criteria used as a basis of reward really reflect the achievement of major organizational goals?

The use of the private sector as a model of good management is not as convincing as it is sometimes made to sound, for experience is mixed. While it is claimed that the large increases in remuneration received by some senior executives are based on objective evaluation of performance, in practice it is often hard to demonstrate that this is the case. There is also the evidence previously referred to, which suggests that performance-based reward systems can lead to an excessive concern with short-term results at the expense of longer-term development. Performance-based remuneration systems can also result in much time and energy going into operating and controlling the system. 'Playing the system' and 'target-manship' become essential skills for individuals who are following the economic dictate of pursuing their own best interest. The ability of organiz-ations to ensure that those individuals are at the same time contributing effectively to organizational goals can be limited.

A note of optimism

Whatever the uncertainties and potential problems surrounding PRP, it is quite clear that local government does not have the option of doing nothing. The traditional system of national pay grades creates no relation-ship between remuneration and either achievement or effort. It therefore provides no motivation or incentive for either. Newly-introduced PRP schemes may not be perfect in the extent to which they directly relate individual and organizational achievements and benefit. They may be based on uncertain and untested principles, and there may be substantial costs involved in designing and operating them. They do, however, at least create some relationship between pay and performance. The extent to which this is achieved will vary from one scheme to another, as will the cost. In addition, as noted by LACSAB, the introduction of PRP in many authorit-ies has led to a much improved analysis, classification and integration of objectives and activities at different organizational levels. That, whatever the other merits or demerits of PRP, is wholly desirable and beneficial to local authorities.

A brief guide to performance related pay schemes

Of the performance-related pay schemes which have been introduced into local government, almost all involve three stages:

▽ defining the performance to be achieved
▽ assessing and rating the performance achieved by means of a regular review process and a specified rating system
▽ making pay decisions in the light of the assessments and ratings given.

In examining each of these stages, much of the information and analysis has been drawn from the extended research programme carried out by LACSAB.

DEFINING PERFORMANCE

There are broadly two approaches adopted to defining performance, the most common of which is by the definition of accountabilities, objectives or key tasks and performance indicators. It is an approach which is identical to that already described in the previous section on performance appraisal, and provides an explicit and clear basis for assessing performance although, as previously indicated, its use can sometimes lead to an over-emphasis on the achievement of short-term targets. The alternative approach, described by LACSAB as 'behavioural', involves the use of standard criteria such as the following:

A. Written and Oral Communication

   B. Organisation, Planning and Control
   C. Leadership and Management Skills
   D. Problem Solving/Decision Making/Judgement
   E. Creativity/Innovation
   F. Targets and Output.

Although these criteria may be supplemented by more detailed explanations
of how they maybe assessed, this method inevitably tends to be less precise
than an objectives-based approach, and it is not therefore surprising that
it is used more by local authorities who have introduced PRP for recruitment and retention reasons than for improving performance.

ASSESSING AND RATING PERFORMANCE

   The degree of sophistication involved in assessing performance, in
order to allocate a rating on which performance payments are based,
appears to vary greatly. All schemes however result in an overall rating,
usually on a five- or six-point scale ranging from 'inadequate' or 'unsatisfac-
tory' to 'outstanding' or 'faultless'.

PERFORMANCE PAYMENTS

   LACSAB identified five different methods for linking pay to performance:

▽ Cash Bonus – percentage of salary is paid as a bonus to better per-
    formers.
▽ Additional Salary Increments – better performers enter an upper range
    of salaries beyond a performance bar.
▽ Higher percentage increases salary – better performers get a higher
    percentage annual pay rise.
▽ Salary ranges – incremental scales are replaced by a new salary range,
    movement through which is based entirely on performance.
▽ Faster Incremental Progression – incremental progression, and number
    of increments, depend on performance rating.
    (LACSAB: Handbook on Performance Related Pay 1990)

LACSAB also identified a number of hybrid schemes combining, for example, cash bonus and salary progression.
   The size of the maximum performance payment that could be obtained
in the LACSAB case studies ranged from as little as 6% of basic salary to
a maximum of 20%. These amounts are small when compared to earlier
manual worker bonus schemes. Even so, in some authorities it was argued
that they did provide a genuine financial incentive. In others the argument
put forward was that the size of the payment was not important, as the
key motivational factor was the recognition of good performance rather
than the payment itself.
   The size of the performance payments, and the new remuneration
package of which they may form a part, have cost implications for local
authorities which have been addressed by using budgetary controls of
varying degrees of flexibility or by placing a limit on the proportion of

staff who could receive payments. In a few local authorities the costs of PRP were included within existing staff budgets without any extra financial provision being made. One reason for doing this was

> to use PRP deliberately as a means of producing savings . . . to force managers to operate it effectively and generatereal improvements in performance.
> (LACSAB 'PRP in Practice' Case Studies from Local Government, 1990)

The cost of PRP to a local authority is also related to the number of staff included in the scheme. The earlier schemes tended to be restricted to a small number of senior managers, but there has been a gradual extension in the numbers and grades of staff who are now eligible. Many schemes now include all staff on principal officer grades (or their equivalent where a new salary structure has been introduced) and in some cases all staff are included. In the latter case it appears common for junior staff to receive a group bonus rather than an individually calculated one. The increased use of contractual methods of management is already making the use of group-based financial incentive schemes more common, and it is likely that there will be considerable further growth in this area. It is likely therefore that the inclusion of all staff in either individual or group schemes will become increasingly common.

What is the effect of PRP on performance?

Mention has already been made of the strong positive and negative attitudes which exist towards PRP and which have to be taken into account in deciding whether and how to introduce it in a local authority. The LACSAB studies have also revealed a wide difference of opinion within those authorities which have already introduced it, but with the balance being very much in favour amongst both employees and managers. The main benefits were expressed much less in terms of the precise motivational effects of payments and much more in terms of the effect of having to introduce well-organized systems of performance appraisal which resulted in a much greater clarification of individual and group objectives, performance criteria and responsibilities.

There is as yet little hard evaluative data which can be used to demonstrate the precise relationship between performance and pay, but it is of interest to note that LACSAB identified a number of ways in which local authorities were attempting to monitor PRP. At the most basic level the cost of PRP is monitored as a budgetary control device. As a means of evaluation, however, the monitoring of costs alone is an inadequate mechanism because of the difficulty in interpreting the reason for movements in costs.

Monitoring the distribution of payments amongst eligible staff is of greater value, allowing judgements to be made about the equity of the implementation of PRP between different groups of staff. The existence of an upward drift in the ranking of individuals and groups can also be used in the absence of other information, as an indication of the process of incipient decay – a process which was characteristic of early bonus schemes for manual workers. Establishing a direct relationship between pay and performance is more difficult and therefore more rare, but LACSAB identified one local authority which was intending to monitor performance payments against a set of performance standards and indicators. Where recruitment and retention is the main reason for introducing PRP it is relatively easy for local authorities to monitor trends using indicators which are already well established.

Evaluating PRP, while important, is a process which demonstrates all the problems involved in evaluating any service or activity in local government. It is difficult to establish precise cause-and-effect relationships. Information is inadequate and can lead to faulty assessment but the attempt to create better information may be costly and create a sense of excessive control which runs counter to the basic aims of the activity itself. The problems of evaluation are not just technical, they are also political in so far as the extent and type of evaluation will be determined by the objectives and interests of the different groups which exercise power within an organization. In the past, many activities have been performed on an 'act of faith' basis in the belief that they contribute beneficially to an objective. While that is becoming less common the increased use of formal evaluation is not 'value-free'. PRP is a value-laden issue and has, at least for the moment, a symbolic value. For many chief officers and councillors it may be one part, but an important symbolic part, of a range of initiatives which are designed to change the basic culture of the local authority. Where that is the case evaluation will be of a broad qualitative nature.

In the short term, while PRP remains perceived as a new and symbolic instrument of change, it is likely that it will be closely evaluated, qualitatively and quantitatively, formally and informally. In other words it will be well managed and changes will be made to individual schemes to improve their effectiveness. It is important that the process of managing and evaluating PRP continues in the longer term, particularly if, as looks likely, it becomes the norm rather than the exception. If it does not, PRP will become a set of routine and bureaucratic procedures and any link between pay and performance, and any motivational impact which may have been created, will be lost.

6 Organizational structure and roles

Outline

This chapter starts from the premise that, because so much time and thought has gone into the constant reorganizations of local authorities, every councillor and senior officer is already expert in the subject. The chapter is therefore a short one, intended to identify some basic principles and explore selected issues.

Out with the old – in with the new

Despite the many reorganizations carried out by local authorities there has, until recently, been a remarkable degree of similarity in their basic organizational shape and form. There are of course many differences, but those differences have arisen within a common framework and the variations, where they exist, have been limited to issues such as the precise arrangement of functions and the structures and mechanisms for achieving corporate coordination. In some cases where reorganizations were carried out they had the appearance of producing a new structure based on the same organizational principles as the old, and therefore amounted to little more than a re-arrangement of the deckchairs.

In recent years there have been signs of more radical reorganizations emerging which have been based on a more fundamental appraisal of traditional organizational principles. The main weaknesses of traditional organizational arrangements revealed by these analyses have been:

▽ *the dominance of the producer role.* Traditional structures and relationships have emphasized the local authority's role as a producer and deliverer of separate services, with the consequence that other roles have been ignored or have formed only a thin veneer over the producer role. The dominance of the producer role is reflected in the structure of committees and departments.

▽ *excessive hierarchy.* Many departmental structures have contained lengthy chains of command, resulting in top-heavy management structures which were not only costly but also tended to obscure rather than facilitate accountability. In many departments the primary organizational principle used appears to have been the provision of career progression opportunities, and while that is a legitimate principle it should not be considered the first or most important.

▽ *hierarchies which reinforce control rather than planning.* In the absence of a strategic planning framework, some senior and middle managers tended, in order to find a role for themselves, to concentrate more on controlling than on planning. This tendency was often reinforced by a bureaucratic culture which was concerned more with mistake-avoidance than success-achievement.

▽ *complexity of structure.* Local authorities have evolved very complex structures reflecting the complexity of their role and the variety of their tasks. The degree of complexity has been difficult to manage resulting in under-laps and over-laps of organizational responsibility for particular activities and policies.

▽ *a lack of assigned and accepted responsibility and authority.* The failure to clarify who is responsible for what in a local authority and to ensure the existence of conditions which support the exercise of that responsibility has been a fundamental problem. It has been represented in traditional job descriptions which made clear what an individual had to do, but not the extent of either their responsibility or authority. It led in many cases to the gradual upward drift of decision-making, resulting from the combined effect of a failure to delegate and a failure to accept responsibility. Nowhere was this better demonstrated than in the frequent schemes of delegation from committees to chief officers which helped to clear committee agendas for only a short space of time, following which councillors demanded the return of delegated powers and chief officers, unwilling to accept their delegated powers, pushed decisions back to committees.

▽ *a lack of direction and accountability.* The opposite tendency in some local authorities was the creation of conditions where committees, departments and individuals were able to become semi-autonomous in pursuing their own chosen goals.

The basic principles for new organizational structures and roles

An organizational structure is basically a way of defining the roles and relationships which need to exist in the organization for it to achieve its primary purpose. Since the purpose and role of local government is subject to change so must, when appropriate and necessary, the organizational structure. As was identified in Chapter 1, changes to the purpose and role of local government are consequent on many external requirements and influences and these have produced a new set of principles and imperatives for structuring local authorities.

1 THE BASIC ORGANIZATIONAL FORM – PYRAMID, MATRIX OR CORE-PERIPHERY

What does your organization look like? The question may seem a strange one, but most organizations are given a visual representation in charts and diagrams which is often one of the first pieces of information which new councillors and staff receive when they join a local authority. This is therefore likely to influence the way the organization is viewed. Traditionally organizations have been represented as *pyramids* – the departmental 'tree' is the typical example – and this form reinforces the view of the organization as being monolithic and hierarchical. Organizations may also represent themselves as *matrices*, with one axis representing the 'line' functions (e.g. service departments) and the other the staff functions (e.g. central and support departments). This form of representation focuses attention on the complex set of interrelationships which exist in a local authority – to perhaps too great a degree, for matrix styles of management often prove too complex in practice to work effectively. The third representation of the organization is one which distinguishes between those *core* staff and functions which are essential to the organization and those *peripheral* staff and functions which are currently performed by the organization but which could be performed by other organizations on a contract or licensed basis. The core-periphery model represents a fundamentally different way of designing a local authority organization, but it is one which is beginning to be recognized as relevant in the context of compulsory competition and in relation to the 'enabling' concept of a local authority's role.

2 SMALL IS BEAUTIFUL

The last reorganization of local government was much influenced by concepts of the economies of scale. Compared to many other countries very large local authorities were created containing large departments organized on the principle of hierarchical control. Thinking in the private and public sectors has changed radically since then, with the acceptance that the theoretical benefits of scale are often illusory because large monolithic organizations cannot be efficiently managed as single entities. As a result many organizations are being reorganized into 'bite-sized chunks' by using principles of decentralization and devolution.

3 LEAN STAFF

The imperatives of compulsory competition have forced local authorities to analyse carefully the cost and functions of central support services and departments.

4 CLARIFYING AND DISTINGUISHING ROLES

There is a greater recognition of the need to define clearly the responsibility and accountability of each member of staff and to distinguish between the main organizational roles of strategic direction, service planning and specification, service provision and monitoring.

5 AN OPEN ORGANIZATION

The need for an organization to have more permeable boundaries in relation to its citizens and a range of other public, voluntary and private sector organizations is gradually becoming recognized. All organizations exist within an environment which influences their activities and which

Contractors

PERIPHERAL

CORE
STAFF AND
FUNCTIONS

STAFF
AND FUNCTIONS

Partners

Core-Periphery

Line Functions

1 2 3 4

A

B

C

D

Staff
Functions

Matrix

Pyramid

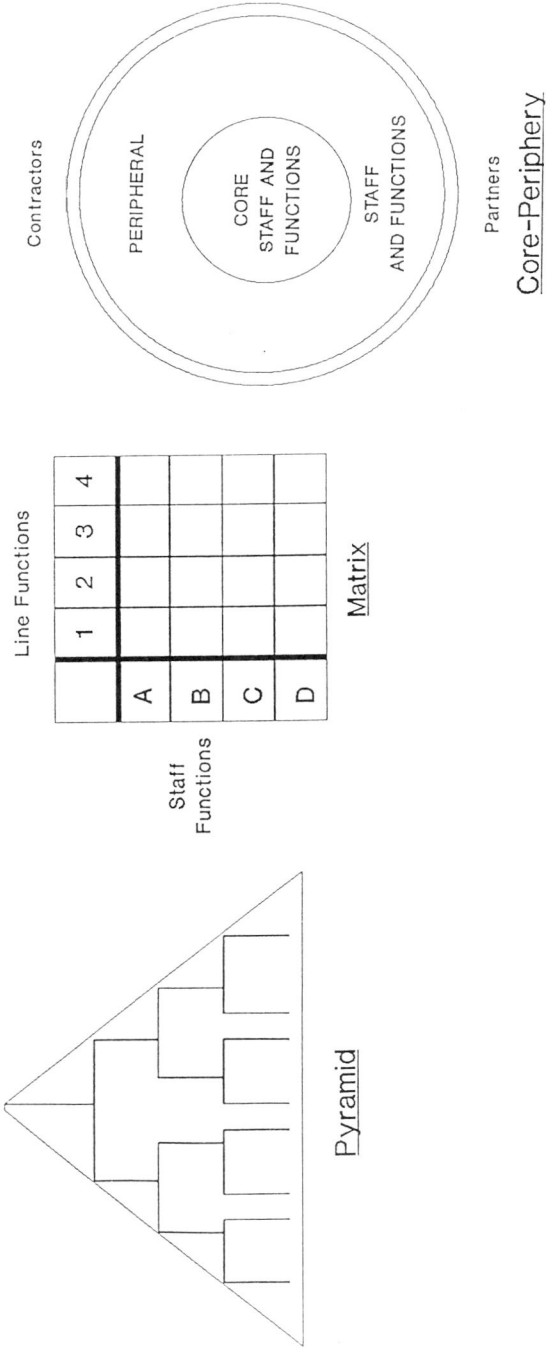

Figure 6.1 Three ways of visualizing your organization

they also try to influence. The way in which an organization structures its relationship with other organizations in that environment, whether it be competitive or co-operative, may be as important as its internal structure.

6 DIRECTION AND PURPOSE

All organizations need an overall sense of direction and purpose which may be provided through an expression of the values of the organization and through a classification of its strategy or key objectives.

Six key questions for thinking about organizational design

The principles outlined in the previous section can be used as a basis for evaluating the design of a local authority. They lead to a number of questions, of which the following are the most important:

1 HOW ARE MANAGERIAL FUNCTIONS TO BE CATEGORIZED AND ORGANIZED?

▽   What are the main categories?
    – Strategic direction and control?
    – Service planning?
    – Service specification?
    – Service provision?
    – Monitoring and review?
▽   How should they be organized?
▽   Where should they be located?
▽   Do they need to be separated organizationally?

2 HOW ARE SERVICE FUNCTIONS TO BE ORGANIZED?

▽   Should there be many departments or a few directorates?
▽   Should departments be organized on a functional and/or geographical basis?
▽   Should service provision be separate from regulatory and inspection functions?

3 HOW ARE FUNCTIONS TO BE CO-ORDINATED?

▽   By using formal rules or shared values?
▽   What needs to be co-ordinated tightly?
▽   What requires only loose co-ordination?
▽   At what points in the hierarchy should co-ordination take place?

4 HOW IS RESPONSIBILITY TO BE ALLOCATED?

▽   What should be the extent of devolution or discretion?
▽   How many responsibility/cost centres should there be?
▽   Should there be few or many tiers of responsibility?

5 HOW IS ACCOUNTABILITY TO BE ACHIEVED?

▽   By means of tight controls?
▽   By clearly specifying individual and group accountabilities?
▽   By independent inspection and monitoring?

6 HOW CAN EXTERNAL RELATIONSHIPS BE ORGANIZED?

▽   By formal arrangements for consultation?
▽   By involving customers in the management of services?
▽   By finding out what citizens think and need?

The questions are only a starting point for analysis, with each question
prompting many more. But attempting to answer the questions is a necessary first step before deciding that reorganization is necessary. Simply
deciding to reorganize as an abstract solution to a number of unclarified
problems is unlikely to be successful.

Four key issues

The main focus of this book is on management processes, and there is
not therefore space to review the many changes which have occurred in
organizational structures. Instead, the remainder of this chapter will look
briefly at just four organizational issues which impact on the way performance is managed.

1 The contract organization

The experience of having to reorganize departments which have been
subject to compulsory competitive tendering is beginning to affect thinking
about organizational design in fundamental ways. In a few local authorities
the basic distinction between client and contractor is being used as a basis
for designing departmental structures. For example, a report prepared for
Cambridgeshire County Council by consultants Kingsley Lord rec-
ommended that the analytical basis for considering the structure of departments should be to allocate all activities into one of three categories:

▽   'strategic buyers' – the client role
▽   'service brokers' – the technical interface or contract management func-
    tion
▽   'service providers' – the contractor role.
    (Cambridge County Council 'Into the 1990s' (1989).)

A similar way of thinking is demonstrated in Arun District Council, where
proposals for the rationalization of the organizational structure of the whole
authority were based on four groups:

▽   The Corporate Core – consisting of elected members, senior corporate
    managers and strategic support staff.
▽   Managing Agents – performing a contract management function.
▽   Contractors – which may be in-house or external contractors.
▽   Support services – which may be in-house or external providers.

A further distinction was made between the first two groups (Corporate Core and Managing Agents) which were classified as 'the Core Authority' and the third and fourth groups which were classified as 'non-core'.

Both the above examples represent the use of the separation of contractual roles as the primary principle in organizational design. Given the immense impact that compulsory competitive tendering has had on local authority structures in very recent years it is not altogether surprising that there should be attempts to translate the organizational lessons which have been learned to other parts of a local authority. However many questions need to be answered about the efficacy of contracting before it can be used with confidence as the primary principle for organizational design. It is only one principle amongst many and is, as yet, an unproven one, as has been demonstrated by recent problems with contracts undertaken by DSOs, the private sector and through management buy-outs. Beyond the question of whether contracts create problems resulting from the inability of contractors to fulfil their contracts, there is also, as Stewart (1989) has pointed out, the potential problem of creating rigidity and inflexibility. To 'design-in' rigidity and inflexibility into organizational structures would be simply to reproduce past failings in a new form.

2 Making citizens and customers part of the local authority

Reference has already been made to the tendency for local authorities to consider themselves as 'closed' institutions having clear and rigid boundaries which define clearly who are and who are not members of the organization. Councillors and officers are considered as members of the local authority and are thus inside its organizational boundaries, while customers and citizens are not perceived as members and are treated as 'outsiders'.

The increasing demands for open government have led to customers and citizens having increased rights to obtain and receive certain kinds of information and to be consulted. While the creation of these rights has been beneficial it does not fundamentally affect the way that a local authority perceives its organizational boundaries – the public, even with their increased rights, remain 'outside' the organization.

There have however been two kinds of development which have had the effect of making the boundaries of local government more permeable. In both cases it is the direct involvement in the decision-making process of either service users or citizens generally which distinguishes them from procedures which involve only consultation or advice.

The first category of developments consists of those which include customers in the planning and management decisions which are involved in producing *particular* services. They include formal requirements such as in the case of school governors, and the creation of management boards to run particular facilities and services, and informal approaches such as the inclusion of social service clients in decisions about the services they should receive.

The second category of development concerns the involvement of citizens in decisions about broad types of decision, usually on an area or neighbourhood basis, and is best represented by the creation of community councils in Middlesbrough, the important characteristic of which is that they have budgets of their own which they use to promote local initiatives.

Developments of these kinds are not yet widespread, and it is unclear whether they have yet led to a radical change of thinking. They do however sit at least on the boundary of local government structures, even if not yet having gained full admittance. Their effect in terms of 'performance' is also difficult to judge, but in making a judgement it is important that they are evaluated in terms of their effectiveness in producing greater public participation in local democracy and in promoting community self-help – which may be considered objectives in themselves – as well as in terms of any improvement in service delivery they may produce.

3 An independent role for monitoring and inspection

One effect of the Government's legislative programme which has already been noted is the prominence which it has given to making the role of inspection and monitoring independent of service provision. Two examples can be used to demonstrate the problems which arise in applying this principle of independence, the first of which is the statutory requirement to appoint a *monitoring officer* contained in the local Government and Housing Act 1989. That officer is responsible for reviewing the legal propriety of the council's actions and procedures and reporting on any action likely to result in illegality or maladministration. To perform that role it may be argued that the monitoring officer must operate, if not independently, at least at one remove from the hurly-burly of executive decision-making. The legislation, however, allows that role to be performed by the new statutory role of *head of paid service*, effectively the Chief Executive role, and therefore the situation is likely to become extremely confused.

The second example is the proposal to set up *independent inspection units* in Social Services departments with responsibilities for registration and inspection of residential care homes in the voluntary and private sectors and for the inspection of all local authority residential care homes. These proposals, first outlined in the 1989 White Paper 'Caring for People', and further developed in a Department of Health consultation paper (Community Care: Caring for People – Independent Inspection Units 1990), envisage a situation where the units will be independent of the line management of local authority homes but will be directly accountable to the Director of Social Services for the exercise of their functions. Apart from the problems of working out the dual accountability role of the Director of Social Services which results – for she/he is also ultimately accountable for line management functions – the important issue in this context is the likely effect on line managers' sense of responsibility for monitoring and reviewing. While the consultation paper suggests that independent inspection 'will be additional to, and will not replace or dilute, the responsibility of managers of L.A. homes for setting, maintaining, monitoring and reviewing standards of care' (Para 1.2) the question of balance and emphasis between internal monitoring and review (i.e. self-appraisal) and external monitoring and review is a critical one. Ensuring that monitoring and review are an integral part of the line management function is an essential principle of good performance management. Equally external, independent reviews and inspections can perform a vital role in challenging established practices which are inefficient or ineffective. The balance between the two is all-important but is often difficult to determine.

4 The role of the centre in performance monitoring and review

The question of whether the monitoring and review function should be seen primarily as an integral part of line-management responsibility or as an external, independent process is also relevant to the question of the role of 'the centre' of the local authority (i.e. broadly defined as central departments) in relation to service departments.

There are currently many changes in thinking taking place with regard to the role of chief executives and the role of the political and officer 'centre'. The changes involve defining the strategic planning and strategic control functions and are too extensive to be dealt with here but have been analysed in other books in this series, particularly by Caulfield and Schulz (1989). The specific issue to be considered here is *whether there is a need for a central performance review unit, and if so, what should be its role?*

There can be no one prescriptive solution to those questions, the precise answers depending on the decision-making processes, style, culture and general structure of the local authority at elected member level and at the corporate and departmental officer levels. However, it can be asserted unequivocally that there is a need for local authorities to have the *capacity* and *capability* adequately to support the corporate decision-making functions of determining strategy, providing a sense of direction, deciding on key objectives and monitoring and reviewing their achievement. Developing that capacity and capability will in most cases require the existence of a unit (or at least an individual) to support the Chief Executive, the elected members and the chief officer's management team. In providing that support the case for having a permanent central unit can generally be expressed in the following ways:

▽   it provides a focus for managing and sustaining corporate performance management systems
▽   it provides a focus for particular initiatives
▽   it enables the local authority to acquire particular skills which are not found in individual departments and which they could not afford to employ on a full-time basis
▽   it provides a location in which certain analytical skills can be integrated in a way which rarely happens when they are located in separate departments
▽   it provides a specific support service for councillors.

The typical weaknesses of central units are:

▽   they can become isolated within the power structure of the local authority
▽   they may lack sufficient knowledge of individual services to achieve credibility and therefore to be of influence
▽   they may themselves lack adequate direction and develop their own objectives and activities rather than fulfilling their corporate function.

Central unit can acquire the characteristic of some research and development units in which the purity of analysis takes precedence over the eventual results.

For smaller district councils there will be the additional consideration of whether a central unit can be afforded in so far as it constitutes an addition to overheads.

Where it is decided to create a central unit it is essential that its role is specified so that both the members of the unit and staff in other departments can be clear as to its purpose and activities, thereby reducing the possibility of uncertainty and conflict. One Performance Review Unit has proposed the following role for itself as a way of achieving clarity of purpose:

∇   Help members set consistent and achievable objectives.
∇   Set up short, medium and long-term targets for individual management groups.
∇   Ensure that new technology is used properly to develop the necessary management groups.
∇   Manage a market research programme to assess customer needs and measure satisfaction with service delivery.
∇   Ensure that the performance of management groups and, where relevant, individuals is monitored against targets.
∇   Communicate the Council's objectives to managers, field staff and customers.
∇   Recommend change.

Providing the necessary support for corporate systems and initiatives does not always require the creation of a permanent unit. In many cases that support can be provided by seconding officers from existing central departments and from service departments to a temporary working party or steering group. Metro Rochdale, for example, when commencing a major corporate performance review initiative, set up a Steering Group of officers, mainly from central departments, which played a major role in designing the performance review systems and procedures. While that system was to be implemented mainly by individual departments, the Steering Group suggested the following advisory, system development and monitoring roles for itself:

∇   Advising Unit Managers on framing of objectives;
∇   Advising Unit Managers on measures;
∇   Advising Unit Managers on systems and databases;
∇   Screening out contradictions;
∇   Undertaking research on relevant experience outside Metro Rochdale;
∇   Progress chasing:
∇   Monitoring the quality and 'pitch' (i.e. relationship with existing practice and level of funding) of objectives and measures;
∇   Monitoring the quality and accuracy of reports on results;
∇   Servicing Performance & Budget Review Sub-Committee.
    (Rochdale Metropolitan District Council: Chief Executive and Town Clerk's Department – Internal Paper 1988)

In a similar way Cambridgeshire County Council established a working group of officers from every department to develop work on performance indicators. By working with departments, and with support from the Corporate Policy and Planning Service and from an outside academic expert, the group achieved considerable success.

Using outside expertise can be a useful way of increasing capacity and capability, and need not be restricted to large-scale consultancies. It can also be achieved by means of:

▽ 'retainer' contracts and relationships with consultants and other outside experts
▽ use of skilled staff from other local authorities
▽ use of advice from local businesses
▽ use of advice or consultancy from other local public bodies (for example, NHS experience with the development and use of performance measurement is of considerable relevance to local authorities).

Questions

▲ *Which of the main criticisms of local authority organizational arrangements apply to your local authority?*
▲ *How do you visualize the 'shape' of your local authority?*
▲ *Try applying the Six Key Questions for Thinking about Organizational Design to your own local authority.*
▲ *Is there a case for a central monitoring and review unit?*

7 The role of councillors

Introduction

The Widdicombe Report on the conduct of local authority business identified the fundamental values of local government as being:

▲ *pluralism*, through which it contributes to the national political system
▲ *participation*, through which it contributes to local democracy
▲ *responsiveness*, through which it contributes to the provision of local
  needs through the delivery of services.
  (The Conduct of Local Authority Business. HMSO 1986 Cmnd. 9797
  p. 47)

The values are stated primarily in political terms rather than managerial
terms, thereby reinforcing the fact that local authorities are governed by a
political process which is an expression of local democracy. It is through
the political process that the purposes and aims of a local authority are
set, and, as a consequence, that the effectiveness of its performance is both
defined and judged. Councillors therefore must have a central role in
determining how the local authority is to perform and in reviewing its
achievements. But an examination of the day-to-day procedures of local
authorities would not necessarily reveal that they do so.

The unclear picture of what councillors really do results partly from
the uneasy relationship which can sometimes exist between politicians and
managers. Councillors may be perceived as a constraint on management
and are therefore held at arms-length as far as is possible – a situation
which is achieved in part by providing them with large amounts of paper
at regular intervals. Those papers, because of their volume, they inevitably
lead councillors into the detail of service management. Thus a cycle is
completed which leads not only to confusion but also to frustration and
conflict. This picture is, admittedly, grossly over-simplified: there are many
other reasons why councillors become involved in the detail of management,
not least of which is their quite proper concern with activities in their own
ward. It does however serve to illustrate the way in which attitudes and
procedures conspire to produce committee agendas which focus attention
excessively on the details of service management at the expense of policy
making and performance review.

Committees dominate the working life of councillors and define their
role within the local authority. The regular cycle of meetings requires a
regular cycle of business to be transacted within which it becomes possible

for the major items of decision-making to become lost because they are undifferentiated from the minor items.

Placing performance on the committee agenda

In theory, at least, it is not difficult to determine the role of councillors within the local authority. It can be defined at three levels:

▽ *Setting strategy and direction, formulating and determining policies and allocating resources* – The constraints imposed by the system for financing local government require that this role occurs as part of an unusual cycle, but it may take place within the context of a longer-term strategic plan.
▽ *Operational Management* – Councillors are responsible for ensuring that there are effective operational procedures which ensure that their policies are carried out. In their role as representatives of their constituents they have a proper concern for the details of policy implementation and service delivery, but this does not mean that they should directly undertake operational activities.
▽ *Performance Monitoring and Review* – Councillors are responsible for monitoring and reviewing both the implementation of policy and the policy itself. The review of policy is to a large extent determined by the annual cycle of policy making and resource allocation. The monitoring and review of implementation varies according to the nature of the issues being considered.

Committee structures and process

Simply asserting that committees should spend less time in the detail of service management in order to concentrate more on their strategic planning role on the one hand and their monitoring and review role on the other, is unlikely to have much effect. To achieve any degree of change, committee structures and processes need to be analysed in some detail. Avon County Council adopted this approach in undertaking a review of their committee decision-making procedures. The results of that review could apply to many other local authorities.

'The main shortcoming of the past is that there has not been a management structure and process in which performance review could operate and the results have been that:

▽ there is the lack of a strong central strategy. Objectives and aims of the Authority and individual services have not been defined
▽ there is a lack of planning for change – and to the consideration of longer term resource availability
▽ output measures have not been fully developed for service planning and monitoring
▽ service standards and performance measures have not always been defined
▽ there is a need for increased investment in the process of strategic and corporate planning for manpower, capital, information systems and finance

▽ there has been inadequate systematic use made of the County profile
   and comparative statistics
▽ there has not been a structured approach to Audit Commission and
   other such external studies which could assist the Economy, Efficiency
   and Effectiveness of the Council's services
▽ project appraisal and post implementation reviews have not always been
   undertaken in a systematic way, e.g. computer systems development
▽ there is a need for a co-ordinated approach to value for money work
   undertaken by Management Services and the Audit Section
▽ the costs and benefits of the existing programmes have not been
   reported to Committee
▽ management information systems, research information and statistical
   techniques which are currently being developed, need to be utilized in
   the best interests of service development and value for money
▽ a corporate pro-active approach to identifying best practice and applying in Avon has not been possible.'
   (D. G. Latham: Avon's Revitalized Performance Review and Decision
   Making Process. 1988)

The analysis resulted in a new policy and service review process, central
to which was the creation of departmental position statements containing
objectives, statements of service standards and levels, and performance
indicators. A new committee structure was also evolved, which was based
on the concept of identifying each of the main decision-making roles of a
service committee, with separate sub-committees, so that each main committee could retain an exclusive focus on policy making. The three types
of sub-committee are:

▽ Policy Advisory Sub-Committees – of which there may be several, with
   each one formulating policy options on a particular topic. The sub-
   committees are intended to operate in a flexible way outside the constraints of the committee cycle.
▽ Policy Implementation Sub-Committee – having fully delegated powers
   to make implementation decisions on behalf of its parent committee.
▽ Policy and Service Review Sub-Committee – having a 'watchdog' role
   of reviewing the policies made by its parent committee and their
   implementation by the Policy Implementation Sub-Committee.

This relatively unusual structural solution, while having the problem of
creating many sub-committees, is a logical response to the analysis which
was carried out. This kind of structural change is one form of solution.
   Applying the disciplines of performance management to the committee
as well as the officer structure is another way in which some authorities
have attempted to create improvements. For example, the London Borough
of Bexley specifies a detailed programme of business for each cycle of each
main committee so that councillors can, from the beginning of the year,
see a clear pattern to their activities. Many other local authorities are also
developing more precise annual cycles of decision making which specify
when key decisions need to be made.
   As the pressures resulting from the Government's legislation increase
in their impact on local authorities, it is likely that they will have to search

for more radical and wide-ranging alternatives to the traditional committee pattern. These might include:

▽ rearranging committee cycles in order to fit the requirements of an annual cycle of key decisions

▽ creating client-group panels to complement service committees, as has been done in Cambridgeshire County Council

▽ creating area and neighbourhood committees instead of, or as a complement to, service committees

▽ having one meeting a year which is exclusively devoted to reviewing services

▽ reducing the treadmill effect of the committee cycle by differentiating between regular meetings for routine business and longer cycles for policy development and performance review

▽ ensuring that every committee meeting contains at least one major review item – placed high on the agenda and not at the end.

A job description for councillors?

Given the many pressures which councillors face it is not surprising that new councillors, faced with the additional burden of having to comprehend the complex machinery of local government, are often socialized into their role in a way which tends to reinforce traditional ways of working and patterns of behaviour. A new councillor who challenges those patterns of behaviour may not always be welcomed by senior colleagues who have a vested interest in the status quo. Nor will it necessarily produce a positive response from officers who will look more to the political leadership for signs of change. Any major change must therefore come from the top, from the political leadership itself, who can clearly indicate that an analysis of the role of councillors is on the political agenda.

Introducing an analysis of this kind is not easy and may require some framework of analysis – a basis for defining what is wrong and what needs to be done. Barratt and Downs (1988) provide a possible job profile for a councillor consisting of eight principal accountabilities which could be used as a framework for analysis:

▽ Constituency needs – informing the organization of constituency conditions and concerns.

▽ Authority-wide policies – contributing to their formulation and review.

▽ Resource allocation – contributing to the determination of resource acquisition and control.

▽ Effectiveness review – participating in review of policies and service operations.

▽ Appointments – performing effectively the duties of any internal or external roles to which appointed.

▽ Internal/External collaboration – secure purposeful collaboration with all relevant groups.

▽ Public relations – promote awareness of policies and programmes.

▽ Personal development – keep abreast of developments and undertake personal training.

In similar fashion Coulfield and Schutz (1989) report on Wiltshire County Council's suggested job description for councillors. Of the twelve items within the job description four relate to monitoring and review:

▽   to ensure the administration of the Council is both fair and efficient, and to contribute towards developing new ways of securing economy, effectiveness, and efficiency in delivering council services

▽   to identify and approve the measures designed to establish the needs of consumers of the Council's services

▽   to keep under review the committee and staffing structures of the Council; to ensure they remain appropriate to the Council's needs; and to attempt to develop flexible structures capable of being easily adapted to changing needs

▽   to ensure that complaints against the Council are taken seriously and investigated properly.

Analysing, and where necessary, redefining the role of councillors is a sensitive issue, being difficult to achieve and therefore easy to avoid. It is nonetheless, in the current climate of local government, an increasingly important and necessary task.

Reviewing operational management

The fact that councillors are responsible for ensuring effective operational management, but not for undertaking it themselves, has already been stated. Differentiating between 'being responsible for' and 'undertaking' is not always easy to achieve, and hence the constant tendency for committees to become enmeshed in detail. One way of avoiding the problem is for councillors to adopt a *Quality Assurance* role as part of which they undertake a regular review of the organizational structure and management arrangements which can be framed around the following key questions:

KEY QUESTIONS/ISSUES

▲   What is the Formal Line-Management Responsibility for:
  ▽   Overall service management?
  ▽   Management of each unit of service delivery?
  ▽   Management of interface between services?
▲   Are Financial, Human and Material Resources Managed in an Integrated Way?
  ▽   If not, do people understand who is responsible for what?
▲   Are Administrative and Support Systems Efficient and Effective?
▲   Who is Responsible for Goal Setting/Task Achievement at each Management Level?
▲   What are the Formal Systems for Monitoring, Inspecting, Reviewing and Appraising the Performance of Individuals and Units?

A community monitor

The councillor can be a monitor on action taken or not taken in the area and an inspector of quality, who can contribute to contract and services monitoring. He or she is a channel for complaints and for the soft data of ideas, suggestions and awareness of what is going on. (M. Clarke & J. Stewart: The Councillor and the Enabling Council. LGTB 1989)

In drawing attention to the role of the councillor as a monitor of the community as well as of the local authority organization, Clarke and Stewart also point out that most authorities do not adequately recognize the role in their organizational arrangements. Not only is the importance which many councillors attach to the role not recognized, it is often rejected and disparaged as 'parish pump politics'. The consequence of such attitudes is to deny the importance of representative democracy in the organizational arrangements of the authority.

There are however many ways in which authorities can, and do, provide legitimacy and organizational space for this role:

▽   area and neighbourhood committees
▽   supporting councillors in holding community forums and debates
▽   providing support and information for ward surgeries
▽   developing systems for handling councillors' enquiries and complaints.

Information for monitoring and review

Much of the information provided for councillors is designed to meet the needs of officers as much as the needs of councillors, because it is essentially the product of information systems and decision-making procedures within the officer organizational structure. Monitoring reports can range from the standardized reporting of one or two routine performance measures to, in one classic case, three pages of narrative followed by fifty-three pages of undigested and indigestable statistics.

To say that the information provided must meet the needs and requirements of councillors is a statement of the obvious and may be countered with the argument that needs vary so considerably that this aim is difficult to achieve. That may be true but it is equally true of a group of officers. Information needs can be defined if the purpose for which the information is required can be defined. Asking councillors can help, as can providing illustrative examples for discussion.

The content of information is of importance too. Reports and performance measures produced from sources inside the authority are important, but so too are those from outside. Public opinion surveys, market research studies and reports from outside bodies such as Parish Councils may all be perceived as valuable by councillors.

Documentary information can be enhanced by the context in which it is given. A review of facilities such as leisure centres can be given more impact by holding it in a leisure centre, and may be made even more alive by involving front-line staff and customers. Inviting front-line staff to review meetings can also enhance the depth and range of analysis.

Performance Review Committee

To have, or not to have, a Performance Review Sub-Committee?

The question of whether a separate committee, sub-committee or panel is required to undertake performance review is raised at regular intervals in a great many local authorities. It appears to be a subject of fascination and never-ending debate, and while in some respects it has achieved a level of importance which it does not deserve, it does encapsulate fundamentally important issues with regard to the role of councillors and the function of performance review.

The key issue with regard to councillors is whether their role is to be seen entirely in *executive terms* or whether their role is also to act as an *independent, political check* on executive action. Within service committees the two roles become confused. Service committees are clearly executive bodies in so far as they determine policy but they also act, formally at least, as a political check on executive action undertaken by their officers. However, because service committees tend to become involved in the detail of determining executive action, the concept of their acting as a non-executive check becomes confused and diminished. One of the arguments for having a special committee for performance review is therefore that it can act in an independent way as a check on the executive function performed by service committees, a role which is reflected in those local authorities who liken their committee to the Public Accounts Committee or Select Committees in the House of Commons. But there are two weaknesses in that approach, the first being that the Public Accounts Committee and Select Committees are not particularly good models for achieving public accountability: despite their investigatory zeal and their ability occasionally to identify issues of immense importance, they remain weak instruments of accountability which frequently find difficulty in obtaining the information they request and in having their questions answered by ministers and civil servants. The second weakness lies in the fact that all members, including those on a performance review committee, have an executive role by virtue of their membership of one or more service committees. The ambiguities resulting from the dual nature of their role become most evident in the workings of performance review committees, and are in large part responsible for the many problems which some local authorities have experienced in finding a satisfactory role and method of working for such committees.

The function of performance review within the management process can also be expressed in terms of whether it should be conducted as an external activity, as represented by the existence of inspectors and advisors in the education service and internal and external auditors, or whether it should be an internalized activity, integral to the act of performing and managing the activity being reviewed, and undertaken by those who are directly involved. The issue is clearly not one which should be expressed in 'either-or' terms – there is a need for both external and internal reviews – and perhaps the more fundamental question to be resolved is that of how the optimum balance between the two can be identified and achieved.

That issue is, however, not explicitly dealt with in the models of management process which underpin many of the approaches to performance management identified in Chapter 4. Indeed their strength lies in the emphasis they give to the function of monitoring and reviewing as an integral part of the management process. The application of this model to the role of service committees is clearly reflected in the Audit Commission's view that:

> Performance review should form an integral part of each member's work for the council, in the same way as it forms an integral part of a manager's job. In general therefore the Commission believes that it should not be hived off to a special group of members or assigned to a separate Performance Review Sub-Committee.
> (Audit Commission: Managing Service Effectively – Performance Review 1989)

The case for integrating performance review with executive action is clearly a strong one, and a performance review committee's existence should not be used as a reason for service committees abdicating their responsibilities for monitoring and review.

But local authorities continue to set up performance review committees and similar bodies, so they must be of some perceived value. They perform a variety of roles of which the following appear most common:

▽ *Determining, implementing and monitoring the authority's corporate systems and mechanisms for monitoring, reviewing and appraising performance* – in this role they do not undertake reviews themselves but ensure that the overall arrangements for so doing are appropriately carried out by others.

▽ *Strategic policy review* – this role may be defined in terms of acting directly as a sub-committee of a policy committee by carrying out that committee's strategic review responsibilities.

▽ *Comprehensive review role* – a role which involves acting as a corporate check on the performance monitoring and review reports which are submitted to service committees as part of a regular cycle of reporting. Items may be identified and 'sent back' to service committees for analysis and action, or investigated by the review committee itself.

▽ *An independent review role* – in this role items for review are independently identified and the reviews carried out by the committee itself. Items may also be referred from service committees for analysis.

▽ *Corporate policy review role* – certain policies cross service committee boundaries and may not have a natural 'home', e.g. equal opportunities policies, policies for under-fives and policies for combating vandalism. In this role, the committee can effectively monitor implementation throughout the authority.

▽ *As a service committee* for those sections, units and teams at officer level, which have a responsibility for monitoring and reviewing, e.g. performance review units, research and development sections and management services departments.

▽ *As a focus for cost reduction and value for money exercises* – this role provides a corporate focus for considering the implications of a variety of such exercises, which may otherwise take place in an unco-ordinated way.

▽ *Capital Programme* – monitoring implementation and reviewing effectiveness.

▽ *Customer focus* – to determine and review the council's strategy for service to, and involvement of, consumers and citizens.

▽ *Complaints monitoring and review* – a role which may be seen as a dynamic way of combining the managerial and 'community monitor' approaches to performance review.

The variety of the roles identified suggests that local authorities use performance committees in quite different ways. This is underlined by the fact that they also use a variety of titles, and many authorities have separate committees to monitor and review the resources of finance, staff and property. The most common role remains that of carrying out a programme of independent reviews, and experience suggests that there are a number of requirements which need to be fulfilled in order for it to be successful:

▽ *Adequate officer support* to ensure that necessary information collection and analysis are undertaken. This usually requires some level of full-time support, but may be achieved by seconding officers from their departments, in which case it is necessary to guarantee that the terms of their secondment ensure that they have time available to support the committee adequately. The role of the chief executive in supporting the committee is of crucial importance and she/he should regard this as a key responsibility.

▽ *Terms of reference* – whatever the precise role determined for the committee, it is essential that this is made clear in its terms of reference. Its powers in relation to service committees are particularly important. In undertaking individual reviews, it is also important to establish precise objectives, which can be agreed with service committees and published within the authority.

▽ *Membership* – some committees have been used as a training ground for new and backbench councillors. While this may be a useful and valid objective, it will make the committee ineffective unless such members are balanced by others with greater 'political weight'.

▽ *Methods of Working* – a performance review committee should not act like a service committee. Its purpose must be to ask questions – to probe, investigate and examine. It should not therefore be regarded as an executive decision-making body. To reinforce this distinction everything possible should be done to make it look and feel as different as possible from a service committee and this might be achieved by:
 – varying the location and avoiding committee rooms
 – having short, perhaps single-item agendas
 – not having a fixed cycle of meetings
 – using small panels to undertake most of its detailed investigations.

Appraising chief officers

As more local authorities introduce schemes of performance appraisal, some of which may be linked to performance-related pay, councillors are more likely to become involved in formally appraising their chief executive and chief officers. Many councillors will not find this easy, particularly where the process of appraisal includes the identification of the officer's development and training needs. In Chapter 5 it was argued that training in appraisal techniques was an essential ingredient in the successful implementation of these schemes, and, in this instance at least, it may be argued that what is necessary for officers is also necessary for councillors. The content and length of training need not be identical – the pressures on councillors' time are likely to preclude more than a brief introduction which should focus on those aspects of appraisal which are most important to councillors. What constitutes 'important' will vary according to the nature of the scheme, but one aspect which will be crucial to all schemes is the setting of key objectives and targets.

Many existing schemes do not directly involve councillors beyond the appraisal of the Chief Executive, who in turn then appraises the chief officers. This approach may be seen as quite appropriate where the role of the chief executive is seen clearly as that of 'managing director'. Where it is not, the logic of the approach breaks down and there are strong arguments for the direct involvement of councillors, provided that the process of appraisal is sufficiently well designed for it not to be abused. Avoiding the abuse of appraisal schemes is not, however, something which is unique to the councillor–officer interface – it applies to all appraisals whether carried out by councillors or officers.

There are two additional arguments in favour of involving councillors in appraisal, both of which are concerned with providing a challenge to existing patterns of behaviour. The first relates to councillors and the dominance of committee membership in their activities. If alternative areas are to be found for them to carry out their role then it may be argued that the appraisal interview is one appropriate alternative. The second argument concerns the general subject of officer-member relations. Where there is a perceived need to improve them it may be argued that appraisals provide one mechanism for so doing because they will require both officers and councillors to consider, and probably reconsider, their existing roles and relationships.

The case for involving councillors in appraisal is not, however, conclusive. There are practical and constitutional problems which need resolving. But the case in favour of involvement does provide a necessary challenge to established patterns of thinking. If the performance management systems described in Chapter 4 are to have a significant impact on local authorities' management it may be necessary for councillors to be as closely involved in the review of individual performance as they are in the review of organizational performance.

Questions

▲ *Do councillors in your local authority have defined roles? Are they clearly reflected in the way decisions are made?*

▲ *In what ways is the community monitor role formally recognized in your local authority?*

▲ *Is there a need for a performance review committee? If so, what role should it have?*

▲ *Should councillors be involved in appraising officers?*

References

Association of Metropolitan Authorities (1990). Response to DOE Consultation Paper – Published Performance Indicators for Local Authority Tenants.

Audit Commission (1986). Performance Review in Local Government. A Handbook for Auditors and Local Authorities. HMSO.

The Audit Commission (1988). The Competitive Council. HMSO.

Audit Commission (1989). Managing Services Effectively – Performance Review. HMSO.

Barratt, J. and Downs (1988). Organising for Local Government – A Local Political Responsibility. Longman.

Burgess, A.A. (1983). Policy Planning Implementation and Review – Synopsis of Seminar Presentation at INLOGOV.

Butt, H. and Palmer, B. (1985). Value for Money in the Public Sector – The Decision Makers Guide. Blackwell.

Caulfield, I. and Schulz, J. (1989). Strategic Planning in Local Government. Longman.

Clarke, M. and Stewart, J. Public Service Orientation. LGTB.

Clarke, M. and Stewart, J. (1989). The Councillor and the Enabling Council. LGTB.

Department of the Environment (1988). The Conduct of Local Authority Business: Cmnd. 9797. HMSO.

Department of the Environment (1989). Published Performance Indicators for Local Authority Tenants (England). A Consultation Paper.

Department of Health Social Services Inspectorate (1989). Homes Are For Living In. HMSO.

Department of Health (1990). Community Care: Caring for People: Independent Inspection Units. HMSO.

Fowler, A. (1988). Personnel: The Agenda for Change. LGTB.

Institute of Personnel Management (1986). Performance Appraisal Revisited: Third IPM Survey. IPM.

Jackson, P. and Palmer, B. (1989). First Steps in Measuring Performance in the Public Sector – A Management Guide.

James, G. (1988). Performance Appraisal. WRU Occasional Paper 40. Advisory, Conciliation and Arbitration Service.

Kline, R. and Mallaber, J. (1986). Whose Value, Whose Money? Local Government Information Unit and the Birmingham Trade Union Resource Centre.

The Labour Party (1988). Quality Street. The Labour Party.

The Labour Party (1990). A Good Deal. The Labour Party.

Local Authorities' Conditions of Service Advisory Board (1990). Handbook on Performance Related Pay. LACSAB.

Local Authorities' Conditions of Service Advisory Board (1990). Performance Related Pay in Practice. Case Studies from Local Government. LACSAB.

Local Government Training Board (1987). Getting Closer to the Public. LGTB.

Mayston, D.J. (1985). *Non-Profit Performance Indicators in the Public Sector*. Financial Accountability and Management Vol. 1, No. 1.

Midgley, J.V. (1986). Arun District Council – Strategic Management 1983–1987. Notes of talk to S.W. Provincial Council Workshop.

National Consumer Council (1986). Measuring Up. Consumer Assessment of Local Authority Services: A Guideline Study. NCC.

Peters, T. and Waterman, R. (1982). In Search of Excellence. Harper and Row.

Ridley, N. (1988). The Local Right: Enabling Not Providing. Centre for Policy Studies.

Spencer, K. and Walsh, K. (1990). Improving the Quality of Local Authority Housing Management. INLOGOV, University of Birmingham.

Stewart, J.D. (1984). 'The Role of Information in Public Accountability' in: Hopwood, A. and Tomkins, C. Issues in Public Sector Accounting. Philip Alan.

Stewart, J. (1989) '*A Future for Local Authorities as Community Government*' in: Stewart, J. and Stoker, G. The Future of Local Government. Macmillan.

Stewart, J. and Stoker, G. (1988). From Local Administration to Community Action. Fabian Research Series 351.

Stewart, J. and Walsh, K. (1989). The Search for Quality. LGTB.

Local Authority Documents

Arun District Council. (1) Strategy Papers and Programme Plans 1987–91. (2) Annual Action Plans 1989–90.

Bolton Metropolitan District Council. Agenda for the 90's.

Bexley London Borough Council (1) The Business Process. (2) Action Plan 1989/90.

Cambridgeshire County Council (1989). Into the 1990's.

Newham London Borough. Area Public Service Statement: South Canning Town and Custom House.

Richmond London Borough. 1988 Annual Management Report Programme: Author's Notes.

Index